Loving, Leaving, and Letting Go

Life With and After an Addict

Meredith Costa

Loving, Leaving, And Letting Go

Life With and After an Addict

© 2021 Meredith Costa

Book Design by Mathew Mondragon

ISBN: 978-0-9968735-2-9

WORDGLITTER PUBLISHING

Dedicated to my former therapist, Kathryn Vernon.

I could not have survived those last two years in my situation without you. You saved my life, and I will always be eternally grateful for all of your help, support, and guidance. I was truly fortunate to have found and had the privilege of working with you. Thank you for helping me find my voice and myself again.

Special thanks to my editor, Zoe Gemelli, for her hard work, and to my dear friend Mathew Ryan Mondragon, who worked so hard helping with the cover and formatting to make my first book absolutely perfect. It's beautiful, I'm so excited, and I could not have done it without you! I love you! Thank you both so much!

Disclaimer

This book is intended to be the story of my experiences with addiction, and a means of information and support for others who are struggling in similar situations. It is in no way intended to attack, demean, or slander anyone. All individuals directly named/mentioned in the following pages gave their consent, and any other mention of individuals involved was kept in generic terminology so as to ensure that identities are protected.

Please do not take anything said in this book as a substitute for clinical guidance and care. I am not a professional, and while I provided a lot of what I hope will be valuable information for those who are seeking support I do not hold any kind of degree certifying my authority to dispense psychological advice or treatment. If you are feeling overwhelmed, depressed, or otherwise unable to effectively manage your situation please seek professional psychological care.

Table of Contents

Loving

1

Looking at him, I knew deep down that he was no longer well. I feared he was past the point of no return. He could barely walk without stumbling, and whereas he had always been a speed walker, now he was barely moving. It seemed like every step he took confused and fatigued him, forcing him to stop for a few seconds before taking another one. His eyes were watery and bloodshot in the corners, and his arms and legs were covered in bruises that he couldn't explain. He had lost control of his bowels in our bed, leaving our blanket destroyed and my greatest fear realized.

As I watched him shuffle into the bathroom and fumble for a piece of toilet paper to wipe the feces off the inside of his leg, shrugging it off as no big deal, despite my urging him to take a shower, all I could do was look at this shell of a man I had once known and loved, and cry. We had been going through this for so long. Drink, self-detox, go clean for a few days, and then the cycle started again. For the last four years, I watched this man that I had fallen so hard for deteriorate and dealt with the monster he became when the vodka made its return yet again. I used to refer to myself as his mistress; the bottle was his wife. He got so defiant when I said it, but our entire relationship was proof.

He had been lucky up to this point that his liver was still healthy, but I feared that that was no longer the case. In the last six weeks, he had had 3 alcohol withdrawal seizures; collapsing, foaming at the mouth, shaking, unable to even tell the EMTs his own name, let alone anyone else's. It's one of the most terrifying things I have ever experienced, and I can remember very few times when I've felt more helpless.

Now here we were in the aftermath of his first drunken accident; a fall down a flight of stairs while I sat here in a panic waiting for him to show up and having no idea where he was or if he was even okay. This time, he completely bypassed the hospital. He was immediately taken to a detox facility where he finally called after I had spent 24 hours beside myself, envisioning him face down in an alley somewhere. He told me he was in the "hospital". No hospital makes its patients use a payphone, let alone stand in line waiting to. That was my first clue that he wasn't at a hospital. It was confirmed when I called the number back and was told it was an alcohol detox facility. Suddenly I remembered sitting in my therapist, Kathryn's office for my first appointment two years ago, exhausted, guarded, depressed, and consumed by fear, guilt, and hopelessness. Talk about an emotional Molotov cocktail!

Now, here I was two years later still fighting so hard to help someone who clearly was not ready to be helped. The repercussions were becoming more than I could handle. I feared that he was dying right before my eyes, and it absolutely shattered my heart to see what this once stable and healthy man was becoming. His body was *shouting* at him for help, and he was blatantly ignoring it, continually insisting he was "fine."

"Sweetie, I'm fine" -- it was a sentence I was so sick of and angered by, because I knew he absolutely wasn't fine. He was barely able to walk normally, in and out of hospitals and detox, and unable to control even the most basic physical functions, and he was still flat out denying that anything was wrong. I begged and pleaded with him to go to the hospital; even offered to go with him. He refused every time instead shelling out more "Sweetie, I'm fine" like he really believed that if he just said it enough, I'd start believing it. Even after all of this, he still insisted that none of the seizures had anything to do with drinking, despite that every single discharge report that was given to him clearly stated "alcohol-withdrawal seizure" as the diagnosis. It was only after the third seizure that they finally admitted him.

Even all these years later, despite how well I knew him, he was still lying to me, which is part of the addict mentality. They don't do it to be cruel (Well, most don't. Certainly, there are psychopaths out there who drugs, and alcohol make that much more evil). It's part of their sickness. Part of their shame. Part of their denial.

Unfortunately, it doesn't make it any less painful for their loved ones who helplessly watch them destroy themselves. Loving an addict is an intense and isolating shackle. We want more than anything to help them, and we twist ourselves inside out and go to great lengths to protect and defend them in the hopes that it will be enough to get them to help themselves. If we can love them enough, if we can give them enough, if we can encourage them enough, that will be all they need to realize that they want help and reach for it. Loving an addict is a lot like being a hostage with Stockholm syndrome. We adapt and learn to love and identify with our addict to survive what we experience at the hands of their addiction. Often, no one even realizes there is anything wrong because, on the outside, we stand tall and don't give any sign or indication that we need help. We become used to what we experience because we fear detachment and separation, as well as of what might happen to them if we walk away. We fear change, or maybe we feel like walking away will be abandoning our loved ones in their time of need.

I know that that's what I've struggled with. I've fought my own childhood abandonment issues my whole life, and because of that, I'm hyper-sensitive to feeling like I'm abandoning someone else. Due to this, I become willing to bend, twist, and damn near break myself trying to support and "help" someone I care about who's in need, even when the logical side of my brain is screaming at me that I'm not helping either of us, I am in fact further enabling the problem.

We can't MAKE them want help. I can't wrap my head around anything worth experiencing seizures like that, but he continued drinking even after the first two, which was his *choice.* As loved ones, we have a hard time accepting that because we don't understand it. Unfortunately, we don't have to understand or accept it for it to be true.. It's a painful truth, but a truth, nevertheless. We sure do put up with quite a lot by convincing ourselves otherwise, though! They need a hero, and dammit, we're going to be that hero if it kills us – and it can!

The single hardest thing for the loved one of an addict to accept is that we *can't* protect them from themselves, and that's the center of the problem. They are *choosing* to use to the exclusion of everything and everyone else. No matter what position we're in, whether the parent of an addicted child, the child of an addicted parent, the romantic partner of an addict, or even just a friend, we can't fix it for them because it's internal. That's the hardest part of setting boundaries with or walking away from an addict. They're still someone we worry and care about, and the realization that we're both helpless and powerless to help them the way we want to so much is utterly gut-wrenching.

Addiction is a brutal captor, and what makes it so much worse is that it's not just the addict who winds up ensnared by its unrelenting wrath. Loving an addict is a special kind of hell, and unfortunately, that's not an overdramatization. Whether it's the parent loving an addicted child, the child attached to an addicted parent, being close to an addict friend, or being in an intimate relationship with an addict, it becomes easy to wind up enmeshed in and by the madness and instability of addiction, and not even realize it until we're often already in too deeply to know how to get out. Loving an addict is to live in a constant state of chaos and stress, which is a terrible state to put our bodies, minds, and hearts into, yet this is where we find ourselves. Whoever this person is to us, we care about them and want to support and help them, and that complicates the situation for us so much more.

Even all this time later, after years of emotional turmoil, instability, hurt, and stress, I still find myself wanting to "help" him. While logically, of course, I recognize that he's a grown man and responsible for his own choices, there is that part of me that wants to rush in to "protect" him and keep him safe. This brings two questions to the forefront: What is it that I'm protecting him *from,* and at what (or *whose*) expense?

Well, I can answer that second question. The expense was mine. It just took me a while to realize it, and the path to that realization was by no means an easy one to find or stay on. The truth was that there were warning signals *very* early on in the relationship. Still, I willingly ignored them because I was so drawn to him and because I myself had an emotional vacancy deep down that I was so desperate to fill that I clung to even the slightest show of affection like I'd die if I let go. We both had some serious internal demons that we battled, and as such, we were pulled to one another as two needy codependents. I can sit here now and say, "Had I known he was an alcoholic, I never would've given the relationship a chance."

The truth is that in the place I was in at that time, I allowed myself to ignore what my mind saw so clearly because he was attractive and charming. He gave off a "bad boy" mentality, which

I liked, and he fed that part of me that had been starving for so long. We got together, then broke up, then got together for what was supposed to be one night and instead turned into four years. Looking back, I should've realized that how destroyed I was when he broke up with me the first time was an unmistakable sign that there was something inside me that was seriously wounded and causing me to need approval and affection so desperately from others because I couldn't give them to myself. I could've spared myself quite a bit of trauma had I been able to see it then, but I just wasn't strong enough nor confident enough in myself at that time to recognize that it was neither right nor safe for me to try and engage in a relationship. I was running from myself. Only now can I freely admit that. I can only now also freely admit that this is most likely why I attracted someone else with severe issues who had no business being in a relationship. More on the relationship between addiction and codependency later, though.

Before I go any further, I feel the need to clarify that in no way am I saying that he was or is a bad person. He absolutely is not and never was. Were we good for each other? Not even a little bit, but that doesn't make him a bad person. His addiction doesn't make him a bad person. That's the thing about addiction; the addict is under the influence of a substance that has the power to change their *behaviors,* and we as a society define personality by behavior, but they are not the same.

At its simplest explanation, personality is who we are while behavior is what we do. It's a bit more complicated than that. Certainly, the two influence each other, but it's particularly important to keep the distinction in mind when discussing addiction. So often, addicts are defined not by who they are but by what they do. They go from being a human being to being a title -- "addict". Even at his worst, he was (and is!) still above anything else a human being. He *has* a condition, addiction, but that doesn't define *who* he is any more than having diabetes, cancer, or depression defines who the person struggling with it is. We wouldn't say a cancer patient *is* their cancer, so why should we define a person battling addiction as being their addiction? Further, it's important to understand that while personality is relatively enduring, behaviors are fluid and change according to experience and situation. While it seems as though the individual's personality has changed, it's important to distinguish that the general characteristics that have always defined who they are haven't *changed* but rather are being *influenced* by the effect of the substance on the brain, more often than not leading to changes in their usual *behavior*.

Still, those behavioral changes can often be alarming and even dangerous regardless of the reason for them. Drugs and alcohol not only lower inhibitions, but they also act on the impulse center of the brain. One study conducted on the correlation between alcohol consumption and violence showed that close to 50% of homicide offenders had alcohol in their system when the offense was committed. Almost that high a percentage was demonstrated to be intoxicated (Vitelli, 2018). If the percentage of violent societal crimes tied to alcohol consumption is so high, imagine how high the numbers are for intimate partner violence in which alcohol/substance use was a factor!

Again, I'm not saying that every relationship in which substance use is present is violent. I am saying that many relationships are damaged and even destroyed by the perpetration of violence due to substance use. Even if physical violence isn't a factor, verbal/emotional abuse is just as much if not more so a likelihood, as well as next to impossible to prove unless it's recorded. Some of the most vicious and hurtful things that have ever been said to me were said by him while he was drinking. From name-calling, to personal attacks, to accusations of infidelity, I spent so many nights crying myself to sleep from the terrible things he screamed at me. These attacks never happened when he was sober. The more he drank, the angrier he seemed to become, convinced that I was doing things I never did and trying to turn his family against him, accusing me of being "psycho" and insisting that my own family didn't know "the real me."

One of my earliest memories of our relationship was me laying on the mattress on the floor of his studio apartment with my back to him. He was drunk and yelling at me about quarters for the laundry, and I was crying. This was long before I realized not only that he had a drinking problem but how bad it was (though really, this should've been a HUGE red flag. Again — my own damaged self-worth wouldn't allow me to let go of the small shreds of affection he did show me). Now here we were, four years later, and I got so used to being yelled at that I first started yelling back then stopped responding altogether (which fluctuated between stopping everything altogether and angering him even more, seemingly depending on how much he had already had to drink). No one deserves to be treated that way. Let me repeat that because it's that important: **NO ONE** *deserves to be treated that way!*

As loved ones of people with addiction, we put up with SO much so that we can keep trying to stand by and support them, and we tolerate far more than most people would in the name of loving and wanting to help them. No one deserves to be yelled at, screamed at, called names, or in any other way mistreated no matter what the reason. Over the years that followed, I got yelled at, called names, and accused of infidelity *a lot* when he was drunk. It broke me down. I stopped caring about myself or taking care of myself. I didn't want to worry those who loved me, so it took me a good year before I started telling anyone anything about what was going on — and that only came about because my twin brother heard him drunk and screaming at me while we were on the phone one night. Needless to say, it worried him; enough for him and my aunt to have a conversation that ended with paying for me to go to a hotel for the night to get away from him.

The "funny" thing about drugs and alcohol is that for as much as they lower inhibitions and make people blunter and even aggressive, they also seem to bring the person's deepest insecurities to the surface; at least that was the case with him. It took me a long time to realize that the things he was so viciously firing at me were actually manifestations of his own insecurities about his past relationships and experiences as well as about himself in general. Drugs and alcohol essentially present the behaviors that reflect the addict's deepest feelings about themselves. They say that alcoholics are the most honest when they're drunk. While certainly, the things they say to loved ones likely aren't true, if you think about it, chances are you can connect what they are saying to you to a part of their own past that would make the deflection far more obvious.

For the last three years of our four year relationship, he constantly accused me of cheating; with men, with women, with every male friend I had who wasn't gay, and even with a stranger whom he insisted I recorded the event with and posted on YouTube... because I was that kind of person that I would demean and degrade myself like that, not to mention destroy my career which was at the time as a probation officer (a position in which reputation is crucial). For the longest time, I took it personally, as anyone would because after all, how could he think I would cheat, and why does he suddenly believe I would be capable of such a thing when he had always known before that's not who I am?! I didn't realize that my reaction further sparked him. His behavior was vodka-fueled and combative, and I was feeding the beast. I had nothing to defend. I had done nothing wrong.

Then it occurred to me --- he had told me more than once that he was chronically unfaithful in relationships including his marriage and that his ex-wife had cheated on him as well. Suddenly the projection became glaringly apparent. How does the old saying go? The more defensive they are, the higher the likelihood that they're doing what they're accusing the other person of doing? Even though I never accused him, he was *very* adamant that HE had never cheated, that HE had always been faithful. Okay... I never said otherwise, so why was he defending it so hard? *Duh!* The point is that whether or not he was unfaithful, these accusations *only* came out when he was drinking. His brain chemistry was so drastically altered by the vodka that he could no longer think clearly -- logically. Again, his insecurities came out, and he lashed (projected) them at me, so suddenly, *I* was the unfaithful one. He was certain that I had cheated on him and was continuing to. It didn't even matter who the accusation focused on. At one point, he was convinced that I had fallen in love not only with someone else, but with someone whom I hadn't seen in five years, was a good four hours away at least, and whom I only spoke with maybe twice a month. On top of that, HE knew this person too. To this day, I have no idea what made him think that this man and I were anything other than friends, but there was no single person in my life at any point during our four years together that he focused his accusations on more than this person. What started as him believing that this man was in love with me (which he never was) quickly spiraled into "We were in love with each other and laughing at him behind his back." What started as an untrue accusation spiraled into paranoia. His mind was so clouded and convoluted by the alcohol that suddenly it was as if there were voices in his head telling him things were happening that never were. His behavior reflected what his severely altered mental and emotional state were telling him. He yelled. He screamed. He told me over and over that if he wanted to cheat, "All he had to do was walk out the door and around the corner and he could find someone.". No matter what I told him, he didn't believe me, and the more I tried to defend myself the worse he became. He slammed doors. He yelled at me from outside on the deck. He went nuts if he thought I was even *looking* at my phone, let alone if I actually picked it up. Every time I did, I was talking to the guy he was convinced I was cheating with. Every time I did, I was hiding something from him. I lost count of how many times he insistently accused me of checking my phone, saying he "saw me" looking at it when either I wasn't even facing the direction my phone was sitting in, or it was clear across the room on the charger. Still, he KNEW I was lying and cheating and became so upset and angry. It reached the point where it had happened so often that it didn't affect me anymore, and I stopped responding to it. That made him even angrier.

When an addicted person is actively using their emotional epicenter is practically on fire because of the toxins and chemicals the brain is being barraged with. More often than not, a person uses to reach that exact place — oblivion, the place where whatever is causing them more pain than they can manage on their own goes away. Unfortunately, what can often appear instead is that heightened state of strong and volatile emotion in which they may not still be being impacted by the original trauma, but by god, SOMETHING is going to piss them off and get them riled up. It doesn't take much because the brain cannot receive and sort logical messages the way it can when sober. Simultaneously, the emotional filter is essentially eradicated, leaving them feeling paranoid, insecure, and ready to take on the world.

Again, this is not intended to be a blanket definition or statement about everyone who struggles with addiction. Of course, everyone is different.

Messages to and from the brain are sent through the body and back via chemical messengers called neurotransmitters, and these messengers are what enable human beings to express emotion. Research overwhelmingly shows that alcohol and drug use surges floods of dopamine, which is considered the "feel good" chemical neurotransmitter in the brain responsible for those feelings of happiness we all try so hard to experience and maintain (NIDA, 2020). These surges condition the brain to seek out more of the substance no matter what the cost in order to maintain that artificial but nevertheless "good" (high) feeling. Conversely, when these messengers are adversely impacted, such as happens with the way drugs and alcohol contort them (NIDA, 2017), we can be left feeling anxious, depressed, angry, and general malaise. Drugs and alcohol play a major role in causing such imbalances, which is why it makes sense that the likelihood of behaviors that exhibit aggression, jealousy, anger, and even violence towards others is sharply exacerbated in those using drugs and/or alcohol. When he was sober, he was a calm, easy-going, friendly person. However, when he was drinking, he became a monster; an angry, unstable, unpredictable, vicious, and hurtful monster.

So, if that's the case — if they are so nasty and hurtful to us, why do we stay? Why did it take me years to finally walk away? It seems on its face like a black and white question with what should be an equally black and white answer. Let me assure you — the question may be black and white, but the answer is anything but. While their illness is apparent, we as loved ones are often sick as well. I had eluded earlier to the hole inside me that I was trying so hard to fill. It would take me years to understand that that hole was called codependency and that codependency is a magnet for toxicity. Codependency is a complex, complicated, and consuming emotional condition that can be utterly paralyzing. When I say paralyzing, I don't mean legs stop moving paralyzed. I mean that the body is spiraled in and out of a constant state of fight, flight, or freeze and codependency essentially locks the person in an enduring and heightened state of freeze. While generally, this response is referred to as "fight or flight", that third response, freeze, is part of it as well. It's a survival response stored in the brain that comes to the surface when fight or flight from a potentially dangerous situation doesn't seem possible. It's one of the brain's responses to anxiety that allows it to disassociate from the trauma to keep the person protected (Seltzer, 2015).

I can speak to this response's reality personally, as I did it *a lot* when the red flags started showing in my relationship. You know that surge you feel in the pit of your stomach when something happens that's uncomfortable, that gnawing sensation that keeps you on edge until the issue resolves itself? Now imagine the body and brain being in that state all the time. All. The. Time. Imagine being gripped by fear and guilt caused by a deep and broken belief that you have to stay in the situation because you can care about and love this person enough to help them get better. This is the feeling that essentially forces you to allow yourself to live in this heightened and uncomfortable state day after day, month after month, year after year, even though you know at your core that the situation is unhealthy in every way possible. That's codependency. That deep-down feeling that we as who and what we are are not enough, and therefore must devote ourselves to the care of others to thereby give ourselves and our lives the meaning we feel they don't and won't have otherwise.

We see broken and want to fix it. We see the pain and want to heal it. We see a need and want to fill it. Peeling back the layers, there is also our own intense need to find, hold on to, and experience that unconditional acceptance and approval that we didn't receive as children, or that we were somehow otherwise deprived of that caused the gaping hole in us in the first place. There are so many codependency puzzle pieces, but the picture at its core isn't whole, and we twist ourselves inside out trying to force the pieces together. We allow ourselves to endure a lot to try and give the love we didn't get in the hopes that if we give enough, we might finally get that return we've craved for so long. Now think of what this could look like when brought into a relationship with an addict. We've all heard the word "enabling." This is the veritable breeding ground for it. I'll go into a more in-depth discussion of codependency and its factors related to addiction in a later chapter.

That "monster" I mentioned earlier — was he born or bred, for lack of a better way of leading into this? There is heated debate surrounding whether addiction is a choice or a disease, and there are a lot of stigmas around it. Some believe it's a matter of genes, while others argue it's a by-product of environment and experience. The American Psychological Association defines addiction as "A chronic disorder with biological, psychological, social, and environmental factors influencing its development and maintenance" (American Psychological Association, 2020, para. 1). So, what does that mean? Let's break it down.

Webster's dictionary defines addiction as "The state of being compulsively dependent on an act or substance that is psychologically or physically habit-forming to such an intense degree that the absence of it is traumatic" (Webster, 2020). This definition in and of itself doesn't offer much clarity as to the possible cause of addiction. The American Psychological Association defines addiction as "The body's need for a substance in order to avoid withdrawal" (American Psychological Association, 2020), while Healthline.com explains addiction as "A chronic dysfunction of the motivation and reward centers of the brain and the compulsion to continue the use of a substance or acting out of a behavior that feeds those centers despite the known risks and dangers" ("What is Addiction?", 2020).

A bit of a wild swing there, but both definitions suggest that addiction is a multifaceted condition and provoked and exacerbated by equally numerous influences. That makes sense, right? It's widely accepted that there is a genetic/hereditary component to addiction; that is to say that the likelihood of addiction's susceptibility becomes heightened by family history (Demers, Bogdan, & Agrawal, 2017). If a parent struggles or has struggled with addiction, genetic makeup dictates that their children will be prone to developing it. Does that mean that ALL children born to parents who have addiction in their past or present will grow up to be addicts? Of course not, but their risk becomes far greater if that is the case.

He had a family history of addiction, so, unfortunately, he was more susceptible to it from the start. Studies show that genetic factors directly relate to at least half of a person's susceptibility to addiction. ("Genetics and Addiction", 2008). For example, there is ample evidence to suggest that alcoholism is at its foundation a genetic disease with variations in a considerable number of the genes that influence the risk of development (Edenberg & Foroud, 2013). This is a lot of psychological wordplay at work. The simpler explanation is that predisposition plays a predominant role in the development and continuation of addiction. Sins of the parents? No. At least in this aspect of addiction, predisposition removes responsibility.

Before anyone looks up my home or email address and starts pelting me with angry messages about giving those with addictions an excuse, I'm NOT saying that they're not AT ALL responsible for their choices and behaviors. While they do not have control over what they're predisposed to at birth any more than we have control over what color our eyes are or how tall we are, this does not remove their culpability for their choices regarding, surrounding, and as a result of that addiction. This is the part of addiction that loved ones struggle with the most, because after all if they can make poor choices and engage in poor behaviors, they can also change, right? Something in their lives drove them to feel that they need to numb the pain by using their chosen substance or the act of their chosen behavior. It stands to reason then that if we can just give them enough love to fill that place, they'll no longer need that substance or behavior. Problem solved!

It's this belief that has entrenched SO many parents, children, family members, partners, and friends in seemingly endless and deeply painful cycles with their addicted loved ones. The unrelenting snare of addiction is as vicious as it is destructive. No amount of external love or validation in the world can or will break that snare. It's an agonizing truth that so many loved ones are forced to come to the realization, and worse, the acceptance of. It's only that substance or behavior that will bring them back to where they feel they can be "okay" again, and they'll do whatever they need to do to reach that place.

Our first Christmas together, his mother (whom I absolutely adore!) gave us a gift card — told him to use it for a nice date-night dinner for the two of us. He, of course, was all smiles and "of course." Still, within ten minutes of us being home, he had taken it from the card she gave it to us in and disappeared, returning a little while later with a pint of vodka and refusing to tell me where the card was because I knew there was still a balance left on it. I never saw it again after that night, but I did see a whole lot of vodka bottles over the next week! It took me making a few poor decisions to trust him before I realized that when he would ask me for my card so he could get cigarettes, that was not all he was getting. When I confronted him about it, he adamantly denied it, even though there was no other explanation for the remaining part of the bills on my bank statement outside of the cigarettes since he never came back with anything else. Still, a pint always suddenly appeared within a half an hour of his return from those walks.

Most people suffering from addictions don't do these things to be deliberately cruel. They're typically not psychopaths who have no regard for anyone else. They *are* willing to be manipulative, though, because all they can think about is getting the substance or engaging in that behavior that will allow them to escape the broken places inside themselves that they're too afraid to confront. If you think about the APA and Healthline definitions of addiction, this makes sense. Does that make it acceptable? Of course not. I used to ask him all the time if what he was doing to himself, not to mention the obvious and severe discomfort of withdrawal were worth it. He always said no, and I believed that there was a part of him that truly felt that way. Still, I also know that he had some severe psychological demons that plagued him. For him, vodka transformed those demons' pain into emotions he felt better able to handle –- more often than not, defensiveness, combativeness, and anger.

Anger is always easier to deal with than pain, right? Well, maybe for the angry person. In reality, it really didn't benefit him either. Still, it was far easier for him to explode in anger over some random thing or stomp around declaring his right to be angry at the world than it would have been to let himself break down and grieve the pain of the trauma that drove him to the bottle in the first place. He wasn't some unhinged and histrionic basket case. When his blood was saturated with vodka, though, he probably could've fooled just about anyone, even within hearing distance, let alone in his presence. He yelled. He ranted. He screamed. He raged. The alcohol distorted his cognition and disrupted his emotional regulation enough to allow him to do so. It really wasn't even a question of *allowing* him to as much as it was that it *drove* him to (remember how I mentioned behavioral changes?). Those inhibitions that we all have as human beings that keep our emotions under control in high-stress times were obliterated by the toxins altering his neurotransmitters.

I remember so many nights spent struggling to block him out enough to get some sleep because he would wake me up suddenly going off on me about something that I had no idea about most of the time. He would insist that I was *pretending* to sleep when he knew I was awake when the irony was that I wasn't even giving him any indication that I was awake in the first place. I was either actually asleep or ignoring him. Still, he took it to mean I was pretending to sleep, though I always told him when I was awake and ignoring him. He would ramble on about my parents, mostly my mother. To this day, I'm not sure what his hang-up was about my mother. He would tell me that he was emailing back and forth with both of them about me and how I "really was. " I knew this wasn't true, but for some reason he believed he could convince me otherwise. He couldn't, but he damn sure tried! He'd say he was "recording" the things I was saying, and sending the recordings to his family so they could "hear the true me." In most of these situations I barely said anything, but he was certain that I had said things that I didn't say. He accused me of texting with whoever he believed me to be cheating with at the time and laughing at him together behind his back, even though my phone wasn't even in my hand. These were all behaviors that never happened when he was sober, but the more he drank, the more erratic, emotionally unstable, and seemingly paranoid he became. I used to refer to the things he said as the messages his "alcohol demons" were telling him because they were just so nonsensical, illogical, and in all honesty, ridiculous. He believed them to be true, though, because his insecurities were running wild with him in his altered state.

Even with this, though, this was easier for him to manage than confronting his trauma would've been for him, which made and kept the motivation to drink so strong for him. That's the thing about substance use — it provides what the addicted individual interprets as a numbing effect, even though it also brings other emotions screaming to the surface. They'll do anything they feel they need to do to maintain that numbness so they can continue to avoid whatever the actuality is that they are running from by using. This provides strong support for the argument that addiction is a choice. They *choose* to lean on the substance or behavior to help them cope with what they are afraid to confront directly. Is it a choice, though, or a compulsion? Is there a difference, and does one mitigate where the other excuses?

Compulsion is defined as an urge, an irresistible impulse to do or get something ("Compulsion", 2021). The drive is so strong that the individual must fight themselves to ignore it and often can't. Addicts are typically explained as having the *compulsion* to use their substance of choice or behavior as they do. Does this mean that they don't actually have a choice? Well, yes and no. It's not that cut and dry, unfortunately. While we always have choices, people who struggle with addiction are driven from just the mere desire to do something to feeling like they have a mental and physical *need* for it in order to feel okay. Do they feel "okay" in reality when they use? Of course not, BUT it takes them away from the true source of the pain, which is typically all they're trying to do, and that's all they need to feel okay regardless of what the picture of that word may look like while they're under the influence. It's that compulsion that drives them to do anything they think they can and need to do to stay in that place. They will lie, steal, cheat, and even commit crimes and hurt people. Are they evil? No. They're running. They're running from pain into that place of oblivion and will execute any means necessary to get there.

Was he evil? Not even a little bit. What he was was in tremendous pain and unable to cope with it. He didn't know how and didn't feel like he had options for how to. Don't get me wrong -– I'm not making excuses for him, but that's the double-edged sword of addiction. Choice or force? Desire or compulsion? Brain chemistry or environmental experience? Certainly, no one can argue that both have influence, but which one is dominant in addiction development and continuation? Which one makes a person more prone to engaging in these unhealthy coping mechanisms? It seems the argument could be made for either side.

The APA uses the word "disorder" in its definition. This is another aspect of addiction that is widely argued both for and against. It would be completely out of the individual's control as a disorder, but does that then mean that they also can't do anything about it? Looking at it logically, no. Many people have disorders that they treat and manage, whether with therapy, medication, alternative solutions, or a combination. So why does it seem so difficult for a person with a substance or behavioral addiction to do the same? Well, I kind of answered that question earlier, but it bears further explanation. Just as a person with a vision disorder wears glasses or contacts, and a person with a deficiency might take medication or vitamins to help regulate it, someone with a substance use disorder can treat it with the same kinds of methods. So why don't they? The simple explanation is that trauma compounds a person's ability to manage their lives in healthy and effective ways. A cop-out? I can see how someone might interpret it that way, but no. It really isn't.

I'm not going to go into the trauma that he endured, the horrors he went through in his childhood. That's neither my right nor my place, and I still care about him too much to share his private experiences with the world. I will say, though, that he experienced things as a child that no child should ever have to go through and were so severe that he and his younger sister went mute for a while and would only communicate with each other. Even after their wonderful and loving mother was finally able to get them out of the hands of their terrible father and even more terrible stepmother and into a safe home, they were so traumatized that when she tried to get them help, they refused to even acknowledge the therapist to the point where she was told that bringing them back would be pointless.

I wish I'd had the opportunity to meet his sister, but she died of an overdose shortly before he and I got together. He and his sister were very close, and her death compounded his demons even further because even though it, of course, wasn't his fault, he blamed himself for not being able to be there to protect her. Anyone with a heart could easily see how all of this trauma might adversely impact a person if they don't deal with it, and that was the problem. He was too afraid of the pain to confront it, so he "medicated" it with alcohol. It couldn't erase the agony and anger he felt when he thought about what he went through as a child, but it could numb it. It couldn't bring his sister back, but it could at least temporarily separate him from the loss. The more he leaned on it, the more dependent he became on the distraction it brought him… and just like that, the disorder was born. I shouldn't say, "just like that", as if it was a foregone conclusion. Still, I think it's important to emphasize how this can happen, how quickly, and *why*.

Can you imagine carrying that kind of emotional devastation day in and day out and feeling like there was no possible resolution and nothing you could do to make it better? I dare say addiction becomes a bit more understandable when put into this framework. Again, I'm not making excuses for him. Just as he knew he had a problem, he also knew there were things he could at least try to do to heal, but the fear of the pain it would come with was too much for him. It was easier to numb it, and that's what he was doing when he drank. Unfortunately, his predisposition to addiction, coupled with his rage at what he had gone through, made him that much more susceptible to movement in that direction. He didn't know how to silence the chaos inside him, so he turned to alcohol to do it for him to both his own detriment and the detriment of everything else in his life. With the drinking came a revolving door of jobs, not to mention a seemingly consistent string of self-detoxification efforts, which looked nearly as uncomfortable and unpleasant as I'm quite sure they felt. Still, it wasn't enough to overpower his need to numb that pain. His mind was so deeply entrenched in and consumed by it that it became necessary for him to make it go away. His brain became dependent on it, and his body followed suit to the point where he became sick when he *didn't* drink. He was addicted; that is to say that psychologically, physically, and mentally he reached the point where he needed it to help him regain what he believed was some semblance of control over what felt like an otherwise uncontrollable situation.

Disorder. Dysfunction. Compulsion. Does this give the addicted person essentially a "get out of jail free" card? Of course not. At this point, it becomes about choice. Does the addicted person get help or continue on the path they're on? While the addiction may have roots in genetics, whether a person confronts and manages it does not. The question becomes how dependent are the mind and body on the substance or behavior's responses? I can tell you that the need that the body can develop on the substance can become severe. Dangerously severe.

In the last months before I made the painful choice to leave, I watched this man who had once been so strong, healthy, and full of life deteriorate into little more than an outer shell housing broken internal wiring both physically and cognitively. His body had become so intensely dependent on the alcohol that he got violently ill when he *didn't* drink. Yet even the doctors at the hospital warned him that if he didn't stop drinking, his body would start shutting down, and I could see it happening. It was one of the most heart-wrenching things I had ever seen. His eyes were pale, discolored, and bleary. His gait was unstable, and he struggled to even stand without stumbling or falling. His hands shook. His body trembled. He was having seizures, accidents, and blackouts. He was sick with the alcohol and sick without it.

His body didn't know what to do with itself. He always spoke strongly against suicide and how selfish he believed it was, but I started seriously wondering if he was trying to kill himself slowly. I knew he was angry and hurting. I begged him to get help and offered to go with him. Time and time again, I begged. Time and time again, he refused.

As many who struggle with addiction are, he was firmly planted in his denial. Frighteningly so. I expect deep down he knew more than he was letting on but was afraid to find out for sure if something was wrong, and he needed to hold on to that denial to protect himself. Nevertheless, this man I loved and cared about so much was destroying himself for the sake of holding on to the one thing he believed could make the pain of his past go away. Even when I implored him to stay with me after having had an accident that resulted in a head injury, he insisted on going to a nearby hotel he had been staying in, knowing that there he would be able to drink. I had set the boundary of it not being allowed in my home, and he not being allowed to stay there if he wasn't sober, and he knew this. His need for and dependence on the alcohol had become so severe that even with a head injury, he preferred to go somewhere alone where he could drink rather than stay where he could rest and heal with someone there to help him. His psychological and physiological need for it overrode everything else. He was homeless. He wasn't working. He had no money. I was footing the bills for his hotel rooms much of the time because of my own need to take care of him (that codependency that I spoke of earlier and will explore in another chapter). Still, as soon as his unemployment payments came through, he was off to the hotel where he knew he had the freedom to do what he wanted without any boundaries, and in this case, what he wanted was to drink.

Making the situation even more frightening, he was getting into fights on an increasingly regular basis. It seemed like every time he went out the door, he wound up in a fight with someone on the street. I'd see the bruises and cuts on his face and body when he came over. He always swore that he didn't start them, that someone tried to steal his cigarettes, or he was jumping into the middle of an altercation in which some guy was beating on a woman. At one point, he told me he was "addicted" to the fighting, and that scared the hell out of me. How could anyone be addicted to being beaten up?! I didn't find out until right before I left that he had been getting into fights for a long time before he met me and that it was something that happened often and only when he drank. The alcohol distorted his cognitive functioning and made him aggressive; it brought all of that anger out that he held in the rest of the time. He fired it at anyone and everyone he came across to get it out.

It had turned him into someone I didn't recognize and often didn't like. He became obsessed with sex, relentlessly pushing me to sleep with him and trying to cajole me into at least having phone sex with him when I turned him down for actual sex. He hit on my friends, telling them we hadn't slept together in a year like that gave him the excuse. He was telling at least one other woman that he loved and wanted to be with her while also adamantly telling me that he loved me and that there was no one else. Even after I confronted him and told him that I *knew* about her — called her by name and told him that I knew of the conversations between them, he still denied first even knowing her and then being any more than just friends with her.

His behaviors became more and more erratic and unsettling. Would he have done such things if he were sober? Never. I knew that. Drugs and alcohol alter the brain's chemistry, more specifically, the part of the brain that processes messages needed to moderate emotional response impulse. The part of the brain that recognizes the potential repercussions of a reaction/response and limits them is severely diminished by the introduction and rush of the chemicals and toxins from the substance being ingested, leading to heightened aggression and diminished capacity for empathy and self-censorship/control. The loved one actively under the influence is not the same loved one we know.

I used to be able to tell without question when he was drunk. Now I was at the point where I couldn't tell whether he was drinking or whether his cognitive functioning was finally starting to slip. This dysfunction, this compulsion, this *addiction* was destroying him from the inside out, and I was utterly helpless to do anything about it. The man I loved was long gone, and I didn't know or even recognize the shadow who remained in the shell before me.

So, is addiction a disease or a choice? I personally don't believe that's a question that will ever be definitively answered in favor of one side of the other. There are strong arguments for both, and clearly, both are influential in the development, exacerbation, and continuation of addictive behaviors. Even if it were to be figured out one day, does it stand to reason then that a "cure" could be found?

I think that that's wishful thinking at best.

I hope one day, someone proves me wrong.

3

January 3, 2019.

Local emergency room.

"How did it happen?"

The question ran a chill down my spine that was so sharp that I shuddered. The doctor wanted to know what brought me to the emergency room just after New Year's Day with pain in my wrist that was so severe that I could barely move it. Did I dare tell her the truth? What would happen if I did? What would happen if I told her that he was in a drunken stupor two nights earlier, and bent my hand back at the wrist and held it in place by squeezing my fingers so hard that they lost feeling and went numb? What would happen if I told her that I spent five minutes tearfully begging for him to let go and telling him he was hurting me before he finally let go? I wasn't even thinking of what would happen to ME if I told the truth; only what could happen to HIM, the man who had just fractured my wrist. What would happen if I told this very kind doctor that this was the first time he had hurt me physically but had been emotionally abusive for the last two years?

I remember hanging my head and quietly muttering something about tripping over the cat on my deck and slipping on some ice, and as she gently wrapped up and bound the wrist that had just been diagnosed as fractured, I felt this sick, heavy, acidic feeling surging in my stomach and wondered for a split second if she might be redirecting her attention to cleaning up vomit in a matter of minutes. As I left the emergency room with my first broken bone ever in 41 years, I couldn't help but feel angry at and even sickened by myself and what I had just done. *Why are you so weak? Why would you let this happen to you and not speak up for yourself?!*

The voice in my head was as unforgiving as it was loud, and as I walked out to my car, passing nurses and hospital staff who smiled kindly at me and wished me well, I felt the tears burning in my nostrils and vehemently choked them back. I sat in my car in the ER parking lot for what felt like hours, just staring blankly ahead of me, my wrist in a cast and tears rushing down my cheeks. I felt lost, overwhelmed, and hopeless. How could he do this to me, and how the hell did I let myself get into this situation? The pain throbbing through my wrist was no match for the pain piercing my spirit. The events of that night played over and over again in my mind like a video stuck on repeat.

I could hear my own voice in my head, pleading with him to let go. I could hear his crazy rantings about my supposed "powers" and "not using them for good" as he continued pushing my hand back, holding my wrist under his arm like he was trying to wrangle a thief into handcuffs. The harder I pulled to try and get free, the harder he squeezed. I couldn't feel my fingers anymore. I don't even remember what finally made him let go, but I couldn't get to the other side of the room and away from him fast enough. I remember waking up the next morning in a state of shock, going through the day like a robot with low batteries. My hand hurt. My fingers were sore and tingling. No matter how hard I tried, I couldn't focus. My mind kept rushing back to it, wondering if he would admit to or even remember it, and fearing going home. Oddly, or maybe not so oddly, I don't remember getting home or anything that happened once I was there. The next memory I have is going into work and having to try to come up with a quick and plausible explanation for what happened because I couldn't type, and my job at the time was 90% typing. I wound up having to quit.

I had mentioned behavioral changes due to substance use. This is another example of that. I witnessed this same behavior minutes before his last alcohol withdrawal seizure, and my stomach sunk. All I could think was, "Dear god, please not again!". Again, he was ranting nonsensically, this time about how he had been "Shot from the apartment across the street," and frantically trying to point out the building he believed it came from. Again, he talked about being hired by "special forces," and that the enemies were "out to get him". Paranoid? Absolutely, but also not in his right mind from the drinking. The bottom line, though, was that he had just physically hurt me. For all the times he swore he could and would never do such a thing, now I knew he was capable of it.

This was my personal lowest point in the relationship, and this was after I had also already endured two years of brutal verbal/emotional abuse --- everything from name-calling, to cheating accusations, to having my best friend's suicide thrown in my face. That's another cog in this multilayered and damaged wheel — addicts can often be abusive while under the influence. Before anyone writes me to jump all over me for making a broad and judgmental generalization about addicts, allow me to clarify; I'm not saying that ALL addicts are abusive OR that addiction will immediately lead to abuse. Everyone is different, and as such, so too will their reaction to being under the influence of their chosen substance be different and unique to them. I'm saying that because of the way substances such as alcohol and cocaine alter brain chemistry, the likelihood of aggression and violence is heightened substantially. Research indicates that incidences of violent behavior and victimization against others are common and even prevalent among those who have substance use problems and that use of substances is directly involved in many violent situations (Brechr & Herbeck, 2013). Adding emotional intimacy to any relationship will naturally elevate the level of intensity within its lines. However, throwing an active addiction into that equation turns an intense relationship into a veritable powder keg with a lit match already attached to it.

I never looked at him the same after that night. I couldn't look at myself the same way either. I had been down this road. I swore to myself I'd never let myself get into a relationship with an alcoholic again, yet here I was. What the hell was it that kept drawing me into them? Drawing, hell, they were *sucking* me in. It was as if there was a flashing neon sign on my forehead that said, "If you're damaged, let me love you," and they did.

June 2000

"I said, come HERE!"

I didn't move. I felt like I *couldn't* move. This was the second time he had told me to come to where he was, and yet I was still standing there in the bedroom, frozen. He was drunk. He was always drunk. Always barking. We had been together for six months, and I had never been with an alcoholic before. As I finally remembered how to move my feet and started towards the room he was impatiently waiting in, I could feel my insides shaking. I saw his eyes before I saw anything else. Hard and angry. Maybe that's why I didn't see his hands flying forward until they were around the back of my neck and yanking me violently towards him. I vaguely remember yelping. I'm not sure if it was out of shock, fear, or maybe both. As he held me by the neck in front of him, I squirmed to try and loosen myself from his grip, but his fingers dug into the back of my neck.

"You're hurting me!"

It was the only thing I could choke out, but I don't think I'll ever forget his response. Even 19 years later, I can still remember it.

"If you had come when I called, it wouldn't have hurt."

The chill in his voice was terrifying, as he made clear that I was to blame for the pain. He squeezed my neck as if to drive home the point before pushing me backward with a disgusted grunt and shaking his head as I hurried back to the bedroom before he could see the tears coming down my cheeks.

Now here I was again, 19 years later. The situation may not have been the same, but it had too many similarities, and I was so angry at myself for being back in this place yet again. How did this happen? What was it about me that drew them in? He was the second alcoholic I had become involved with in 19 years, but by no means was he only the second unhealthy man. Unfaithful. Emotionally bankrupt. Sociopathic (THAT was a fun one! Looking back, I think it'd have been less painful to sit on a porcupine while having hemorrhoids). You name it, and I dated it. Healthy and stable, however? Nowhere to be found. So, what the hell was going on? Remember that codependency thing I talked about? Yeah. That's what was going on. I just didn't know it at the time. I could've saved myself a WORLD of heartache and trauma if I had.

From a young age, I felt unlovable. Messages family gave me told me as much. Criticizing. Judging. Telling me the things I could change about myself to make me "lovable." God, my poor friends. I was an emotional train wreck by the time I reached my early 20s, constantly needing validation, and bless their patient hearts; they did their best to give it to me. That relationship with the first alcoholic demolished what little self-worth I had left, but the problem started way before that. I was deeply ashamed of my gender due to messages I was given as a child that I was born the wrong gender, I hated my body because my family told me that I needed to change it if I wanted to be loved. I developed early, so by age 13, I had been sexually assaulted.

All my life, the message I got was that I was not enough. All I can say is thank god for my father and twin brother. They are the reasons I didn't kill myself when I was 13. I tried. My father had always taught me that no one and nothing is worth my life, and I couldn't bring myself to put my brother through that kind of pain just to end my own; otherwise, that wrist-slicing attempt would probably have been successful. I was so desperate for someone to tell me I was lovable and enough. That's how codependency is born. I became so painfully attached to any man who showed me even the slightest affection. I had one friend, Justin… I honestly don't know how this poor guy tolerated me. He showed me some affection and BAM! I was obsessively attached to him. We never had a relationship beyond friendship, but I became unable to recognize that. Therefore, I absolutely crumbled when he got involved with someone because of the sudden loss of that unconditional affection he been giving me. He hadn't abandoned me, but I sure felt like he had, and it was the most devastating feeling I had ever felt. In reality, he hadn't done anything, nor ever indicated in any way that we were more than best friends. We had become close, though, and there was affection between us, and that was all that hole inside me needed to cling to him as a child clings to a favorite toy. *I* was unable to recognize the line between best friend and girlfriend.

All I could see was the affection. First, it was there, then it was gone and worse, being given to someone else (because she was obviously more worthy of it — at least that's how it felt to that codependent wound), and yet again, that hole inside me interpreted that to mean I wasn't enough. Good enough. Smart enough. Pretty enough. Just… enough. I was 23 years old… nearly 20 years ago, yet I can still remember crying uncontrollably and the pain that consumed me when I found out he was dating someone. The poor guy. He really did have the patience of a saint. Amazingly, 20+ years later, we're still friends. Our friendship isn't the same. We don't talk the way we used to, but I'm happy to see him happy, and I'm grateful for everything I learned from him and that relationship as it was at the time. So, that was enough for me to realize that something inside me needed help, right?

Well, you would think so anyway.

That's the thing about codependency -- it's as covert as it is unrelenting until you consciously acknowledge it's there and needs to be confronted so it can heal. You don't necessarily understand *why* things like this feel like rejection and abandonment and hurt so intensely. You only know you hurt -- a lot. You only know that whenever any source of that acceptance and approval that you're so desperate for goes away or even changes, the pain is so severe that it can literally become difficult to breathe. You're sure your heart is going to explode and kill you… you may even hope it does. That's how intolerable that gaping, bleeding, painful hole becomes. You finally found that unconditional affection and acceptance you've ached for your entire life. You're *finally* "enough" for someone, and then suddenly it's gone, and you're left feeling abandoned and worthless all over again. That codependency — that trauma bond (another term I will explore further as we go) immediately reverts to the initial abandonment -- the initial wound and reacts not to the current situation as a healthy individual would but as the wounded part that was never healed. Codependency is painful and brutal and makes it impossible to have healthy relationships with others. That deeply wounded inner part is in constant search for what it needed but never got that caused the wound in the first place. We don't love; we attach. That's not to say that we can't or are not capable of love. Of course, we are. It's just that that wound of need overrides everything else and inevitably clings to the slightest hints of what it perceives as finally getting what it needs. That attachment is so intense that it becomes a need, and when the source we deem as supplying to that need is ripped away, we're left bleeding and feeling abandoned and worthless all over again.

Okay, I've talked a lot about codependency, but what I've explained so far is really only one side of it. There's another element of it that is both crucial to and typical of a relationship defined as codependent — that being that the other person has to be in some way emotionally unavailable, which is what drives the codependent individual to try *so* hard to "take care of them". Naturally, this warrants further explanation. Think back to the addicted person. Having an addiction would make them unable to be present and healthy in a relationship because their focus is the substance or behavior they're addicted to, right? The codependent sees the addicted person as someone in need, and they become determined to provide for that need - not the need for the substance but the need for that addicted person to be taken care of.

For the codependent, this is a two-fold fulfillment. They are taking care of someone else (need #1 — they are taking care of someone else in need because they themselves don't feel worthy enough on their own, so they find that "worth" in the caregiving of the other person). In turn, they hope (and even expect) to receive that love and appreciation (validation) back (need #2). They try and try and try, twisting themselves inside out to "help" (otherwise known in the realm of codependency as "rescuing") their loved one. Meanwhile, they keep waiting for that unconditional acceptance and love that never come, because how could they? Whereas their priority is their loved one, their loved one's priority is their substance or behavior. Something else to consider is an individual with a disorder such as a personality disorder. For example, can you imagine how someone could torture themselves trying to "love healthy" someone with Narcissistic Personality Disorder? A person with NPD will be cold, critical, grandiose, self-entitled, and demonstrate a constant need for validation (Mitra & Fluyau, 2020). While the codependent would certainly be all too willing and able to provide that validation in droves, they will never get their own need for affection and validation met because their loved one is incapable of it. That won't stop the codependent from damned near killing themselves trying, though; thus, codependency's cycle is born and continuously perpetuated.

The more rejected the codependent feels, the harder they will fight, and the more they will give to try and regain the initial hints of affection and acceptance that they perceived to have gotten in the first place. Granted, the picture is different for family members, but the premise is the same. Unmet need for acceptance + unavailable loved one = codependency. Through that neglect, the child is taught that they are not worthy — not deserving of love, because after all — if their own parent doesn't care about them, why would anyone else? A child doesn't understand the mechanics of addiction. They only know that mom or dad doesn't pay much attention to them, or, conversely, the only attention they get from that parent is yelling, screaming, devaluing, etc. Their emotional development essentially grinds to a halt because the needs at that developmental stage were not met. From this point forward, as the child grows, moves through adolescence and into adulthood, if they're not able to recognize and address the initial source of the trauma, they will continue to seek out that validation of worth that they didn't receive from their parent in equally emotionally unavailable people.

It's no secret that adolescence is an extremely turbulent developmental period. Can you imagine what that wound could potentially lead to on top of all of that natural hormonal instability?

By the time the person reaches adulthood, they are so filled with self-loathing that they don't know how to engage in healthy relationships because they struggle to accept or even understand how anyone could love them just for them (that feeling of not being enough). God knows I can speak to this!

Until I was well into my 20s, I couldn't for the life of me understand how anyone could love me for who and what I was because the message I had received from crucial adults in my world as I was growing up was that I wasn't worthy. I constantly needed my friends to tell me that they loved me or show me that affection, because when it didn't happen I felt like I was being suffocated by a force I couldn't see. That's why when Justin started dating someone, I crumbled. Even though there was no intimate relationship there, his affection and approval had fed that place in me that needed it so badly. In this case, he wasn't available simply because the feelings weren't there, and my codependency was driven by my false interpretation that there was a relationship there simply because he was affectionate towards me and told me he loved me. Sure. Friends do that. I tell my friends I love them all the time. Healthy people also know and understand the difference between platonic love and romantic love, or in the family system, they can distinguish between boundaries and rejection (the same could be said for healthy people in romantic relationships, but for the sake of separation between the two it was an appropriate differentiation). Codependency is where that understanding becomes broken and severely disrupts the person's ability to function in healthy relationships because of that intense need for validation Coupled with the inability to accept others' boundaries, which the codependent personalizes as rejection, they are often spiraled into desperate efforts to hold on so as not to lose what is so painfully needed inside them.

There are still many parts of codependency that need further exploration to paint a clear picture of this painful condition's ferocity and the other person's role in the relationship when that other person is an addict. One of the most significant factors in Codependency is a term that I mentioned earlier — trauma bonding. I think this is an important place to start, so let's look a little more at it from both sides.

4

February 2019

"I can't abandon him. He has been through so much in his life. I don't want to be one more person who abandons him.".

I could see the worry and concern on Kathryn's face. I saw it the second she called me into her office and saw my arm in a cast. It took some pulling to get the truth out of me. She knew I hadn't slipped on ice, but I was determined to try and convince her otherwise. Unfortunately, my tears gave me away within seconds of my effort to choke the story out. At this point, the relationship had gone from verbally abusive to violent, and she feared it would continue to escalate. I had experience working with victims of domestic violence. I knew she was right to be concerned, and yet there I was, trying to explain and even somehow defend what he had done to me.

"That does not give him the right to hurt you. I'm worried he will escalate".

I adamantly shook my head, tears now spilling down my face as I gingerly cradled my fractured and cast-wrapped wrist with my other hand. Everything she was saying made absolute sense, and I knew it to be a genuine concern, yet the thought of walking away caused a pain in me that made the tears come even faster. This man had just physically injured me, but I couldn't abandon him. After all, he did love me. He said it, and there were times when he showed it. I also knew that he had lost so much in his life, and I knew how being abandoned felt. I knew how terrible it felt to feel like no one cared about you; that you didn't matter anymore. How could I do that to the man I loved?! I wasn't in denial about the likelihood that the abuse could escalate. I was refusing to accept that it was not my responsibility to ensure that he wasn't alone or that he was taken care of. I love him; therefore, I'm supposed to take care of him.

"I can't turn my back on him. Without me, he'd have no one. He'd be homeless".

"Without me.". There it was. I believed that not only could I save (rescue) him but that it was my *responsibility* to. Further,

this statement was proof that I believed that he couldn't take care of himself. Here he was, a man in his 40s, and I was assuming that he'd be a helpless child who would surely falter and fail without me. Pretentiousness? On the outside, it may appear that way, but it really wasn't. I saw someone in need, and I jumped. I recognized a need in someone else that I never got met myself, and an opportunity to (what I interpreted as) "fix" it – fix *him*, while also getting those small "doses" of affection he gave me. Affection in the form of physical touch. Affection in the form of appreciation. Affection in the form of praise. It didn't matter. It was affection, AND I made myself more worthy as a human being by taking care of someone else. How can that go wrong?!

Oh, but it can. So, *so* wrong. I'm not in a healthy place. He's not in a healthy place. I'm feeding a need (or what I perceive as a need) rather than providing the kind of natural love with boundaries that healthy relationships come with. He's feeding a need and his addiction, but that's what makes him emotionally unavailable to me and unhealthy. Unsafe. Those minuscule "shots" of affection he gives me, however, are enough to keep me locked into this otherwise wildly unhealthy relationship, fighting, struggling, tangling myself up trying, thereby thickening that bond further. That's a trauma bond.

The *Trauma bond* is a concept first coined and explored by Dr. Patrick Carnes in his book *Betrayal Bonds (1997).* In its most basic definition, the trauma bond refers to a relationship pattern characterized by attachment to a toxic partner, in which cycles of affection (validation) are interspersed with typically more prevalent patterns of abuse, invalidation, and mistreatment (Leigh, 2019). There is so much more to it, though, as evident by the fact that not everyone who has a toxic person in their life struggles to cut ties and escape. Those small " shots" of affection that I mentioned play a crucial part in maintaining and strengthening the trauma bond's knot. Looking at the very term itself, we can better understand how the trauma bond works and its causes. Consider that unhealed wound I talked about, and what it needs to feel attended to; that slightest bit of affection and what it does to that empty and painful place. Now think about it as it could relate to empathizing and developing a connection with another person who's struggling. Not only does the codependent feel at their core worthless and define their worth by their ability to care for others, but those random experiences of affection from the ultimately unavailable partner further "feed" that place so intensely that the codependent becomes willing to do anything to hold on to that feeling. They become desperate to keep those bursts of affection coming, despite how random, inconsistent, and even minimal they often are, because to lose them would be to be abandoned again, thereby resolidifying their initial feelings of worthlessness. The trauma bonded individual will endure the most terrible and even unforgivable of mistreatment and abuse for the sake of holding on to those little glimmers of approval, even though there's no guarantee of when or even if the next one will come, nor how much or little there will be to it. Will the reward be worth $1,000 or $1? It doesn't matter, as long as it comes. Dr. Ramani Durvasula, who is the brilliant and world-renown expert on Narcissism, describes the trauma bond as a slot machine ("What is Trauma Bonding?", 2020), and it's the perfect analogy. You never know how much reward you'll get or even if you'll get one at all, but for the trauma bonded individual, the risk is worth the pull just for the *chance* to get some of that unconditional positive regard that they crave so desperately. Meanwhile, they're getting mistreated, gaslighted (another term I'll further explain), and even abused. Their relationship is chaotic and uncomfortable, but this is how they have learned to define love because of that unhealed wound stemming from their own unmet need.

Certain characteristics also shape the trauma bond right at the beginning of the relationship. While naturally, the beginning of any new relationship is exciting, it's like being struck by emotional lightening for the codependent. The intensity is sharp, immediate, and powerful. Yes, it's exciting but not in the healthy "Oh, hey, I like this person! I'm excited to get to know them better and see what can happen!" way. It's far more like "Oh my god, I've found my true love! This is going to last forever! It's like magic!", even though they still barely know this person. It's intoxicating (only a partially ironic choice of words in this case) and consuming. Finally! That source of unconditional positive regard and affection! In these unhealthy relationships, this feeling is typically perpetuated and continued by a behavior called love-bombing. This behavior is characterized by one person being showered by signs and displays of affection and adoration by the other person in the relationship. Gifts. Promises for the future. Praise. These are tactics used to manipulate, but the codependent person only sees and, more importantly, *feels* the affection even though it's only surface deep. This is generally behavior demonstrated by narcissists, but it's not difficult to see why an addict might engage in it as well.

When he and I first got together, I was *stricken*. Absolutely stricken. He told me I was beautiful. He told me he had loved me from the moment he first saw me. He spoke of the intimate moments he wanted us to share. He called me the sweetest pet names. He texted me night and day, everything from "Good morning, beautiful. Have a great day. I love you" to "I can't wait for us to be together finally.". I felt as though I was flying a million miles above the earth, and he was keeping me soaring. I would sit anxiously by my phone waiting to hear from him and become very anxious and nervous if a certain amount of time went by and I still hadn't. Here was this charming, confident (little did I know how wrong I was on this one!), strong, and, to me, also absolutely gorgeous man who could have any woman he wanted, and he was pursuing *me!* When we met, he was not in a place where I could have become easily aware of his alcohol addiction. I saw a man who had been handed an unfair and unfortunate hand in life but was doing what he had to do to make it better for himself. He had a steady job, went to the gym, and took care of himself. He was making the best of a crappy situation and doing what he had to do to get back to where he wanted to be. The sound of his voice caused this surge in the pit of my stomach that I couldn't get enough of. Even the way he said "Hey," when I first answered his calls made my knees buckle.

My feelings and how much affection he showered on me overcame me so much that I ignored the red flags that popped up even early on; the times he snapped at me on the phone for something trivial or because I did something that he didn't think I should do (I " didn't listen to him" –- red flag! Red flag!). The night he told me how "drop-dead gorgeous" his ex-wife was and that he'd "never feel for me the way he felt for her", and then got huffy and dismissive when I reacted with hurt feelings, questioning why I was so hurt and telling me I was too sensitive (Gaslighting!). "Okay," I thought to myself, "well, this is still new for both of us, and he's feeling unsure. I'm sure he didn't mean it the way I took it" (It was MY fault that HE said something hurtful. Self-devaluation. Typical codependent thinking). I let myself overlook it because I was so infatuated with him and because it seemed so minimal compared to the affection and adoration he showed me. So, the cycle began. At this time, we were still living in separate states, so I'd not yet seen the full picture.

That would not remain the case.

October 2016

**_"Your family doesn't know the REAL you; how crazy
you are! No one is ever going to want you if I leave! I can see
why your ex's leave you."._**

He was drunk, as usual, and yelling at me again, as
usual. We were homeless and staying in hotels. I was not typically
one for spur-of-the-moment decisions, but this cross-country
move was exactly that. We had talked about moving back to my
home state where my family was, and it was very much a case
of, "Let's just go." We packed up what we could of his tiny studio
apartment into the back of my car and left that same day. I didn't
tell anyone, nor did I say goodbye to anyone; a decision that
almost cost me my best friend, who was extremely hurt when he
found out I had left without even telling him I was going. He didn't
talk to me for two months after that. I remember the night he
yelled and screamed at me about how selfish I was. I just sat
there in tears trying to get him to understand, but _what_ was I trying
to get him to understand? I had just done something completely
erratic and out-of-character without saying a word to anyone and
didn't even call him until we were in Ohio. I was in love, though.
Why couldn't he understand that and be happy for me?! Maybe
he saw how unhealthy my behavior was?

Now here we were going from hotel to hotel, never
knowing if we were going to have a roof over our heads that night
until I confirmed that I had booked at least a few more nights. We
had settled in for the night, and I don't even remember if he had
already been drinking by that point or if he had bought the vodka
once we got settled in. He was raging, yelling, and screaming. I
don't even remember why anymore, but I remember finally fleeing
the room in tears and heading outside onto the front lawn of the
hotel where I called my sister, who was understandably alarmed
and concerned to hear me crying when she answered. This is
what many of my memories with him consist of –– him drunk,
screaming and yelling at me for what seemed like whatever
reason he could come up with at the time. I'd love to sit here and
say that I have an emotional library of happy memories with him,
but honestly, those kinds of memories are as few and scattered
as they are bittersweet. So, with a picture this grim, it should have
been easy to leave, right?

For a healthy and logical person, yes. I was neither of
those at the time, however. Why could I not break away? Why
was I so painfully consumed with guilt at even the thought of

walking away, which I saw as abandoning him? Why were those small glimmers of affection — a kiss here, an "I love you" there — why and how could they possibly be enough to keep me glued to this relationship in which there was so much instability, chaos, and mistreatment?

Trauma bonding. I was trauma bonded to him. My unhealed wounds — that codependency that I spoke of had opened up a painful need inside me that I searched desperately to fill, and it was that place that *identified* with HIS past suffering and saw him as someone I could "love healthy" because I knew how it felt to feel unworthy. The love-bombing was all that place needed to cling to him as a child clings to a favorite stuffed animal.

Fast forward a year later, and things had gotten so much worse, yet I was still there. He was still yelling and screaming, and now, he had started accusing me of infidelity, and it had reached the point where the accusations were almost daily. He'd say horrible things to me. He threw my best friend's suicide in my face. Admittedly, I think I've blocked a lot of it out because he was just so emotionally vicious when he drank. Then, a few hours later or the next day, he was all affection again, telling me he was sorry and that he loved me and hated when we fought (so did I, especially since for at least the first year and a half of the relationship the yelling was largely one-sided; at least until I finally reached my breaking point with it and started yelling back). My codependency solidified that trauma bond, and every little bit of that intensity; that affection and positive regard I got from him reinforced and tightened it further (think that scenario I referenced earlier about never knowing when or how much the reward would be but going back for it anyway). That inconsistent reinforcement kept me attached, despite the horrible treatment that, were it happening to a friend of mine, I'd beg them to get away from as fast as they could. The relationship was in all ways toxic, but the thought of leaving it and leaving him caused a pain in me that was so overwhelming that it eradicated leaving as an option.

He promised he would get better. He promised we had a future together. He promised he loved me. These promises kept me holding on, even though the logical part of me very clearly saw that his priority was his addiction. He would beg me not to give up on him. That was a trigger for me. I knew how it felt to be given up on, and here was this man I loved and cared so much about pleading with me not to do the same to him. How could I even think about it?! This is how trauma bonding works. Affection is given in inconsistent ways and amounts, promises are made that are never kept, and we know deep down that this situation we're in is unhealthy, but we can't bring ourselves to leave. Instead, we fight harder to try and "help" (change) the person and gain some control of the situation.

So, if you think you might be in a trauma bonded relationship, here are some questions that you can ask yourself to understand it better so that you can determine what your next steps should be?

- Did the relationship start intensely? Did it feel "electric", like "magic?" Did you feel immediately drawn to and by the person?

- Did this person lavish you with affection early on in the relationship? Gifts. Praise. Adoration. Did they tell you they believed you were "the one" or that you two were "meant to be?"

- Did the relationship move quickly? Did you move in together within months of the start of the relationship? Did you begin making plans for the future right away? Did this person talk about marriage and the wonderful life you were going to have together before you two even really got to know one another?

- Did you begin to notice instabilities and inconsistencies in the relationship that, when you brought it up to the person, they were quick to make promises of change?

- Did the affection start to become more sporadic, even though the relationship's chaos seemed to remain constant?

- Have you had fights — the same fights over and over that never seem to find a resolution?

- Have the people in your life begun to express concern about what they see from the other person in the relationship, but even with these concerns, you still can't bear the thought of leaving?

- Do you feel stuck, like you're not sure which way to go in the relationship or like no matter which way you go, it's going to result in the same outcome?

- Have you tried to leave only to experience so much pain and discomfort that you feel like if you don't go back, these feelings will destroy you?

This seems like a lot, I know, but there's nothing simple about trauma bonding. As such, unfortunately, there is nothing simple about breaking a trauma bond, either. It's easy for people on the outside to say, "Just leave! Why don't you just leave?!" It's always easier to judge something from the outside of it, though. If just the *thought* of leaving this person in and of itself causes us such unbearable pain that we immediately dismiss it as impossible, what would it feel like to actually *leave*? What would that physical separation do to us? I can tell you that it's not an easy place to be but having said that allows me to now give you hope to follow that up. As someone who has been going through it for the last five months — it *IS* doable, and you *WILL* begin to heal. I will be going into further depth on this later on in this book. Just know that if you do leave, even though it will hurt, that hurt will not last forever, and it brings with it a gift once you're able to see through the darkness to recognize it. Please also know that it takes a tremendous amount of courage and strength to break a trauma bond, especially if you're able to go and remain in no-contact with this person, which is really the only way to heal from the trauma. Again, more on that later.

It is critically important to stop here and say that what I have just laid out should not be considered as a suitable outline for relationships in which there is physical abuse. Violent relationships are typically risky to escape from, and I don't intend for anyone to take anything in this book as a guide for what they should or shouldn't do. If you are physically unsafe, I urge you to reach out to domestic violence resources, law enforcement, and anyone else who may be able to help you. Let me start by providing the National Domestic Abuse hotline number right here:

1-800-799-SAFE (7233).

It is a 24/7 hotline that can provide you with resources and further help wherever you live. It's an invaluable tool for getting safe from an abusive relationship. I also urge you to please be careful. Leaving a violent relationship often heightens the risk. Please be sure that you have all you need in place to ensure that once you're away and safe, you'll be able to stay that way. Your safety is priority, no matter what. If it is safe for you to leave, and you feel you're ready, then, by all means, do it. You've got this! If there has been violence in the relationship, however, please be and remain mindful. *Safe* escape is the most important thing.

I'll be honest — before I left this relationship, I had never heard of trauma bonding. I knew plenty about codependency because, after all, I'd been living with it for probably longer than I could recall at that point. I first learned about trauma bonding in a group that I had joined on Facebook that offered support to past and current loved ones of addicts. "*Trauma bonding?*" I remember thinking to myself, "*That sounds like something far more severe than what I'm going through. I feel for people who struggle with that*". The more I read about and researched it, though, the more eerily and uncomfortably familiar it began to feel. The more sense it started to make, and the more correlation I saw between the signs of trauma bonding and the relationship I was mere days out of, complete with my second attempt to go no contact in less than a year. I didn't want to see what was right in front of me.

I had *identified* with his trauma. I had instantly *attached* to the *intensity* of the relationship from the beginning of it. I *held on* to the *small bits* of *affection* he gave me, even though I never knew *how much or little,* or *when* they'd happen, or even *if* they would. We always fought about *the same issues,* but resolution never remained. He *promised* me he would get better and that we would have a future together, but nothing ever changed. I could see the cycle, but I didn't want to face it. I didn't want to have to admit it to myself. Even if I did, I couldn't leave him. The thought of it made me feel like I'd die inside. I had practically been a walking billboard for trauma bonding! The realization hit me like a smack in the face. It made sense, perfect sense, and I hated it. "*How could I have let this happen?!*" I berated myself. "*I swore I'd never become involved with another addict, never let myself be abused again, and yet here I am!*".

Let myself? Did I just blame myself for the abuse that I had endured?! I did. We often do. We need to find some way, any way to try and make sense of what we've been through, and all too often, it winds up coming down to us blaming ourselves just somehow to make the otherwise illogical and confusing feel clearer. The truth is that trauma bonding does not afford us a choice. It's part of an attachment pattern born of unhealed wounds. The only way to avoid its malicious grasp in the future and recognize an unhealthy relationship before we get into it is to work on ourselves and heal that deeply wounded inner place so that it is no longer the foundation we reach out from when seeking companionship with others. Again, easy to pay lip service to and much more difficult to do but recognizing what and why is a critical first step towards healing it.

Two years. It took me two years, some deep emotional wounds, and a fractured wrist to finally break that bond with my addicted former partner. During that time, I separated from him for a few nights at a time many times and even kicked him out once, but I always let him come back because the guilt overrode everything else. The ache of the separation was relentless and overwhelming, with intense emotional collapses that I swore I wasn't going to be able to get through before they passed. That pain was about the worst I'd ever felt, second only to the pain of losing my best friend to suicide. It was that pain that kept driving me to let him come back, the pain and the guilt. The promises were always made, but nothing got better. They only continued to get worse. He was hiding bottles all over the house, then trying to convince me that I was the crazy one when I called him on it. The fighting got worse. His aggression came out. The infidelity accusations continued. Even with all of this, though, I still couldn't bear the thought of leaving.

That, my dear readers, is trauma bonding. Painful, relentless, and seemingly unbreakable.

As I said earlier, though, have faith — because it's not. Difficult and uncomfortable to break? Absolutely, but not unbreakable. Please know, believe, and trust that. I can speak to this personally, and I will.

5

"Please, sweetie. I'm asking you to do me a solid".

This was something I heard on what came to feel like a recording stuck on repeat. "Do me a solid," "Do me a favor," or "I'm asking you to help me.". Anytime he wanted something that he couldn't get for himself, these were the things I heard. In the beginning, I gave in to him... otherwise known as *enabling* him. It didn't take me long to at least cut off the alcohol gravy train (one that never should have gotten on the track to begin with, but I digress), but it hardly stopped there. The most common request culprit was cigarettes but extended to taking him places or picking him up from places at all hours, buying him something if he couldn't afford it, and even calling his bosses for him to make excuses for why he didn't show up for work. I was a full-fledged enabler. I was willing to do anything he claimed he needed in my desperation to hold on to those little crumbs of affection. What I was really doing was making his life more comfortable by doing things for him that he could and should have been doing for himself as an adult.

Enabling. This is a dynamic referred to regularly in the addiction community because it's all too common. Codependents are notorious for their tendency to enable, largely in the form of caretaking but also in other ways, such as the one I described. When talking about addiction enabling means that the individual continues to try and "fix" things for the addicted person, rushing in to shove the pillow under them so that instead of hitting the rock bottom that most addicts need to hit to finally seek recovery, the "blow" is softened. The addict remains sheltered from the consequences of their actions and choices. It's an easy cycle to fall into, and as with most things healing-related, it's not such an easy cycle to break. Codependency makes it even more difficult, because of that driving need to take care of others. The more we do for others, the more worth we're able to find in our own existence. People who suffer from addiction are a bottomless pit of need.

That's why they seek substances or other behaviors that are addictive. As discussed in an earlier chapter, the substance or behavior allows the addicted individual to escape the pain they're in because they cannot do so themselves. The pain is so great that they fear trying to face it. Now here comes the codependent, also from a place of unhealed pain and trauma and looking for something to give them the worth they cannot feel on their own. They see the struggle that the addict is going through, and they want to help. They want to make things better. They want to *rescue.* They believe that this is their purpose; to "save" the addict. They take it as their personal responsibility to do so, from that place of empty need. They believe that taking care of this person struggling so hard will fill that empty place because the addict will return all the love and devotion they're giving them. I don't mean that to sound like the codependent is selfish. That's really not what it is and certainly not what they're functioning from. Like the addict, they're trying to ease their own inner pain, in this case by turning their entire focus onto taking care of someone else in need.

If I do all I can to take care of this person who is struggling so hard, I can help them get healthy again, and my life will have meaning. This is most likely what someone who suffers from codependency will tell you they were thinking, and feeling should you ask them what made them stay with their emotionally unavailable and even abusive loved one. They unwittingly perpetuate the addict's cycle not necessarily by directly providing the substance, but rather by making the addict's life as comfortable as possible, typically thereby drastically reducing or even eliminating the necessity for the addict to take responsibility and accountability for their actions and choices because they will always have someone there to catch and essentially clean up after them. The codependent wants to feel love and worth so desperately that they will twist themselves inside out, trying to stay ahead of the addict to help them avoid repercussions that could in any way be uncomfortable or destabilizing for the addict. Meanwhile, their own lives become increasingly destabilized by the chaos of trying to take care of an addict; a person who is incapable of being present in healthy ways in any relationship but will gladly accept anything that anyone around them is willing to do for or give them so that they can maintain focus on ensuring that they can always obtain their chosen substance or engage in their chosen behavior.

Of course, the codependent isn't *trying* to make it easy for the addict to continue using. In their minds and hearts, they're *helping* this person who's going through so much and struggling so much. The codependent becomes the adult they didn't have taking care of them as a child now taking care of the child (the addict) who can't take care of themselves. The addict has a need, and the codependent wants so much to fill that need. The codependent also has a need. Giving that unconditional positive regard and love to the addict fills the need to feel worthy by devoting themselves to another's care. They also get those "bits" of approval and positive regard they need from the addict in the random, inconsistent, and uncertain signs and gestures of affection even though they never know when it will happen or how much or little they will get. They need and crave it and hang on through anything to get even that slight " fix.". For codependents, that's what those minuscule gestures of affection are — their fix, just as the substance is the addict's fix. The codependent tries to " love" the addict healthy again, but the addict does not prioritize the relationship in the same way the codependent does. That's not to say that the addict doesn't care, because oftentimes they do. They're driven by their addiction, though, and that drive is their primary focus. How can a person with such a fierce force inside them possibly have left what is necessary to create and sustain a healthy and stable relationship?

I mentioned the word *enabling*. So, what can, and often does it look like within the constructs of a codependent relationship/relationship with an addict? Honestly, the ways are pretty endless, but there are some common ones. Let's explore them. Ask yourself if any of these behaviors sound familiar in your relationship.

Of course, the most obvious enabling behavior is helping the addicted individual obtain their chosen substance. At the beginning of my relationship, he would ask me to "do him a favor" and buy vodka for him. I was already so drawn in by him and to the relationship that I would do anything to keep the intensity of it alive. He needed a "favor." He asked me for "help." How could I refuse him? I was already deeply entrenched in my codependency, and the relationship had become so intense so quickly that I felt emotionally overcome; blindsided. It's accurate to say that I was essentially addicted to the feelings, that emotional "high." As such, I was willing to do anything to make him happy, and he knew that. He was willing to manipulate that to get what he needed. I'm not saying that he was some cold and callous monster, but he *was* as entrenched in his addiction to alcohol as I was to that feeling of emotional euphoria. Thankfully, I was able to recognize what I was doing fairly early in the relationship and stopped. Naturally, this did not sit well with him.

He got upset. He tried to guilt me. He begged. He, of course, threw those words around — "favor," "help," "solid" — those trigger words that he knew had always worked on me in the past. Those were the words that touched that unhealed wound in me that found worth and fulfillment in what I saw as opportunities to help (take care of) others in whatever form seemed to be needed at the time. "Need" is also a tricky word here because the argument can easily be made that the addict doesn't *need* the substance and would even be better off without it.

This looks absolutely true on the outside, but keep in mind the earlier exploration of addiction's power on the body and brain. A "need" is defined as something that an organism requires for survival, producing an adversarial outcome if not obtained. *Producing an adversarial outcome if not obtained.* This is the key here. Let's first consider this in terms of basic human needs. What happens when a basic human need isn't met? A person without access to food becomes hungry and can even die if they cannot feed themselves. What happens when a person loses their job? Loss of income can often lead to the inability to meet a host of other basic needs — the ability to pay for shelter and food, the ability to tend to medical needs, ability to provide for oneself and one's family. These are all adversarial outcomes to loss of ability to meet needs.

Now, think of need in terms of addiction. Withdrawal is the body's response to the loss of the presence of something it has come to require. As much as addiction is mental and cognitive, it's also very much physical. What happens when the body goes for days or weeks without water, food, or sleep? It becomes ill and unable to function until whatever that deprivation is gets fulfilled. It's very much the same with addiction. The body becomes so used to the substance's presence because of its constant use that if that substance suddenly becomes absent, the body reacts the same as it would with prolonged loss of food or sleep — illness. I can speak to this first-hand. I witnessed the violent way his body reacted when he would go into his self-induced detox periods. Vomiting, shaking, chills and/or overheating, exhaustion. His body had become so used to the toxin of the alcohol that it responded to its absence as deprivation of a need. Think about that for a minute. His body became so used to having the alcohol that it responded with violent illness when it *didn't* have it. There it was - the need. I would often ask him if what he was doing to himself was worth it, and he always said no, yet I lost track of how many self-imposed detoxes he attempted. Sadly, they always resulted in the same eventual outcome: relapse. The relapse is the response to the body's *need* for that substance. That need is refed, and the illness abates at least until the next time. In this context, it becomes easy to see how addiction is perpetuated.

Back to the enabling behavior – I saw this "need" in him, and my own need responded. That need was the one that required I take care of someone else to feel worthy, and in turn, continue to receive that affection that that place inside me was so desperate for. I heard those trigger words -- "need," "favor," "help," and that place inside me jumped into action to see to it that he got what he needed. For the first few months of our relationship, I ensured that his life remained quite comfortable.

Alongside the alcohol, he also constantly used those trigger words to get me to buy him cigarettes. Over the course of even the first year of the relationship, I easily spent hundreds of dollars on cigarettes for him because he would be unemployed yet again and ask me for that "favor.". Was he manipulating me? Absolutely. Did I know somewhere in the back of my mind that what I was doing for him really wasn't helping him? Yes, I did, but the more overarching motivation for me was that caretaking drive born of and fueled by my Codependency and the trauma bond that had formed so immediately. All I could consciously acknowledge was that this man I loved "needed" something, and I had the means to provide it. I was giving him the resources and environment required for him to continue feeding his addiction. I was *enabling* him.

Enabling isn't by any means solely restricted to providing the substance for the addict. If you think about it in terms of what I just said about making and keeping life comfortable and providing resources, the enablement picture broadens considerably. For example, cigarettes may seem like a small and meaningless thing but consider how this can make for a more conducive situation for the addict getting what they need. What does the addict ultimately need to obtain their substance? Money. While $7.00 or $8.00 given for a pack here and there may not seem or sound like a lot, that's $7.00 or $8.00 that is free for the addict to use towards that substance. With $7.00, my ex could easily buy at least one pint of vodka. At $3.99 a pint, he would need just a handful of change to buy two. Over the course of a month, at a pack, every 4 --5 days, that $7.00 or $8.00 adds up to a significant amount spent by someone else, and more importantly, a significant amount that the addict doesn't have to spend and can now use to get more of their chosen substance. In my emotional blindness, I didn't see what was happening right in front of me. Clearly, he still had *some* money, and every time I brought a pack of cigarettes for him, he had that money free and clear to buy vodka. I put the brakes on doing this for him, too, after allowing him to use my card to buy a pack led to him coming home with a pack and a pint. Up to this point, though, I was making life comfortable for him and providing him with a resource — money — that *enabled* him to then continue using whatever money he obviously had to get his substance.

Let's look at the larger picture of enablement, going back to those basic needs, food, and shelter. You might be thinking, "Everyone needs those and would prioritize them." You would think so, yes. For me, this particular scenario wound up reaching far beyond just allowing him to stay with me so that he would have a roof over his head. Even early on in the relationship, he could not maintain his own apartment because he couldn't hold a job and used the money he did make on cigarettes and vodka. I moved out at one point in the relationship, and he rented a new apartment in the same building. Within two months, he was evicted for not paying the rent. It was only because *I* had a positive and consistent relationship with the landlady that she chose not to charge him for the rent he owed. Instead, he just allowed him out of the lease with no financial repercussions. He was fortunate that she was as kind as she was.

After this point, he moved back in with me, and this began what became a vicious cycle of struggling to keep a roof over both of our heads while he contributed minimally to the bills. I don't say this to disparage or bad-mouth him, but I think it's important that the whole picture be clearly painted to explain the potential reach of enabling behaviors fully. From the hotels we had to stay in in the three months we spent homeless once we returned to the apartment I was finally able to rent, I paid most of the bills. He paid a cable bill or a grocery bill here and there once we were in the apartment, but it was sporadic, as was his ability to maintain employment. What there always seemed to be a surplus of, though, was vodka. He would get a job, work for a few weeks, get paid that first paycheck on Friday, and by the time he got home Friday night, either he was already buzzed on his way to being drunk, or he had the bottle hidden away somewhere and would chug on it throughout the evening. Within two hours of being home, he was drunk. In the beginning, *I* was the one who would leave, spending money to stay in a hotel for a few nights just to get away from him when he was drunk. Meanwhile, he was comfortable back in the apartment that was in my name, drinking until he passed out without anyone there to hold him accountable. *I* was leaving my own home and staying somewhere else while *he* was allowed to stay there and continue doing what had driven me out. I was *enabling* him to keep drinking.

At some point, I finally realized that I was not the one who should be leaving, and I started making him leave. That was the end of the problem, right? Not even a little bit. Yes, I was telling him he had to leave; however, I was also *so* worried about his safety and felt *so* guilty because I felt like I was abandoning him (my codependency in full control!) that to ensure he didn't have to sleep on the street I'd cough up a few hundred dollars in a stretch to put him in a hotel. While I may have been holding him accountable, I still wasn't allowing him to face the consequences of his behaviors. I was protecting him because I was still so firmly entrenched in that caretaking role. I was rescuing him. Continuing to *enable* him to use. After a few months of this, I let him come back amidst promises that he would get help.

This is perhaps the single most typical part of the addiction cycle — promises of change to the loved ones. It didn't get better, however. Very little actually changed, and when change did happen, it was fleeting at best. Even after my leasing agency found out that he was living there and not on the lease and told me he had to leave, I still did all I could to ensure that he remained off the street. I felt obligated to take care of him. I couldn't even begin to estimate how much I spent on hotel rooms over the course of our relationship because the cycle kept spiraling: Let him come back, he'd drink, I'd tell him to leave and put him in a hotel, he'd tell me he missed me and wanted to come back and that he would get help, and so it continued.

The one thing that always remained a constant was the vodka. Here I was spending hundreds and hundreds of dollars to keep a roof over his head, and he was free to use what money he did have to supply his addiction. I had only good intentions in what I was doing. Ultimately, though, I enabled him to continue using by ensuring that he had a safe and comfortable environment that he didn't have to worry about paying for. While he did help with groceries from time to time, he also knew that the kitchen was always stocked and that I would ask him what he wanted me to get for him when I did the ordering. I kept things comfortable and expected very little back from him. A better way to put that would be that I felt guilty — *guilty* at the thought of setting those boundaries that would come with the expectation that he *regularly* helped with bills and household needs. Boundaries are a painfully difficult practice for codependents because, again, they don't feel that they are enough as a person even to have, let alone express their needs from or expectations of someone else. Not only could I not bring myself to set a boundary that would remove him from my home, but I couldn't even insist on a financial contribution from him if he were going to be allowed to stay. It wasn't until I started setting and *maintaining* those boundaries with him that I really saw a change. For three years, I continued to let him come back, help only minimally, and keep falling back into the drinking cycle because of that overriding compulsion inside me to rescue. I continued to *enable*.

There are so many other ways enabling can occur. It's an easy trap to fall into and a far more difficult one to climb out of, let alone stay out of. Some other ways to enable can include:

- Bailing a loved one out of jail after an arrest related to the chosen substance or behavior.

- Driving the addicted love one around, thus relieving them of the responsibility of having to figure out their own transportation arrangements. God knows I was guilty of this many times over!

- "Letting things go" or issuing a consequence for a behavior and then not following through on that consequence.

- Making excuses or covering for the addict and their behavior.

- Paying bills or providing other financial support for the addict.

- Offering to use with the addict in the belief that it will strengthen the relationship (That may sound insane, but if you think about the way codependency impacts the mind and emotions, it makes the picture far more believable).

- Finishing tasks that the addict was supposed to complete.

- Continuing to give chances, even though promise after promise made by the addicted loved one is broken.

- Prioritizing the needs of the addicted loved ones above and beyond all else.

- Not expressing feelings to the addicted loved one out of fear of their response.

- Blaming yourself or others for things that are really the fault of the addicted loved one to "protect" them.

This is not an exhaustive list by any means. Unfortunately, there are endless ways that enabling can happen, making it so difficult to recognize and stop. These are the primary ones that most often occur in relationships with addicted individuals. As a recovering codependent, I can tell you that though many of these probably sound like common sense not to do, common sense is next to impossible to engage when you are heart-deep in a relationship with an addict. We don't want to abandon them. We don't want to "leave them hanging." We want to help them. It's important to keep in mind the difference between helping and enabling, *especially* when talking about addiction.

The difference between helping and enabling is that helping is doing something or assisting someone in doing something that they can't do themselves. Enabling is doing things for someone that they are not only perfectly able to do and are capable of, but also *should* be doing for themselves. Paying bills. Maintaining employment and housing. Caring for oneself. Under normal circumstances (meaning not due to a force beyond the person's control, such as a natural disaster or diagnosis of serious illness), these are daily routines of care and survival that functioning adults should be able to do for themselves. By doing these things for the addicted person, we are basically giving them silent permission to continue using because they feel confident that we will step in and ensure that they remain safe and comfortable no matter how much they use or how much they hurt us. We're telling them that we will clean up after them when they make a mess due to their addiction and that they will not have to take any accountability for their behavior. The less we hold them accountable, the more permission we're giving them to continue using. It's a struggle for us because we want so much to do what we feel will help them, but we're doing exactly the opposite. It's a tough reality to learn and accept. This is where we need to learn how to draw and maintain boundaries — another challenging thing for a codependent.

6

October 2019

"Please! Please! Please! Meredith! Meredith! Meredith! **Meredith! Please! Please! Meredith! Meredith, please! Meredith, please!"**

This had been going on for nearly an hour. It was almost 11:00 pm. He was drunk and out of cigarettes. I had to be up early the next morning for work and was in my recliner trying to get to sleep. He was kicking the extended footrest, trying to make the chair jerk to get me to stop ignoring him. The more I ignored him, the louder he got until he was yelling my name.

"I KNOW you took them, so you should buy me a new pack! Please! Please! Please! Meredith, please! Meredith, please! **Meredith, please!"**.

The sound of his voice made my insides clench, and I could smell the vodka on his breath even from where he was standing at the foot of the chair. That unmistakably stale smell made my stomach turn. I had no idea where his stupid cigarettes were, but he was adamant that I had taken and either hidden or crushed them, so I owed him. He often misplaced things when he was drinking and made an equally regular habit of blaming or accusing me when he couldn't find whatever it was. Usually, it was his lighter. This time somehow, it was his cigarettes, and he was practically having a tantrum because he couldn't find them. Of course, it was as it always seemed to be in his mind *my* responsibility to fix it. This time, however, I had refused and was not relenting. He was convinced he could change that because he had always been able to before. I always eventually gave in because I struggled with that sinking guilt that all codependents tend to battle when telling someone else "no." Here it was 45 minutes after the initial accusation, though, and he wasn't getting anywhere, which was continuing to fuel his anger. He started kicking the footrest even harder, and I was worried he might break it, but I also knew I couldn't give in to his fit.

"I said *NO,* and I'm not going to say it again!".

I spat it out through grit teeth, kicking myself even as I gave him even that little bit of verbal acknowledgment. I knew it wouldn't somehow suddenly make him realize he wasn't going to get anywhere and stop, but I felt driven to reinforce the boundary that I had been maintaining for the last 45 minutes despite his defiance. I could be as stubborn as he was, but this wasn't about stubbornness. In the back of my mind, my own voice was screaming all the things I wanted to fire back at him — how his cigarettes weren't my problem and how if he weren't drunk yet again, he'd probably know where the damn things were, but I knew that that would only fan the flames and encourage him further. This wasn't about fault or having the last word. I had said no, and I knew I needed to stick to it no matter what he did to try and break me. His eyes narrowed, and he leaned in and hovered over me. I tensed, not sure what he was going to do, and I was thankful it was dark enough that he probably wouldn't be able to notice it. He was too drunk to notice much of anything anyway, but I also knew he was angry, and that drunk and angry was never a good combination.

"I KNOW you're awake! Don't pretend you're sleeping!".

My eyes were open, and again I was thankful it was dark so he wouldn't see me roll them. He did that a lot – accused me of "pretending" to sleep when I stopped verbally acknowledging him. In the beginning, I'd immediately shoot back that I was wide awake and ignoring him. Then I realized that that's what he wanted because it kept the argument going. He stood up again, and I let out the breath I had been holding in to avoid breathing in that god-awful vodka stench. For a second, I considered reaching down alongside the chair to snatch up my wallet out of my bag, but I was still hoping that if I just stayed still long enough, he would eventually assume I was asleep and stop trying. Wishful thinking, to say the least. He started kicking the chair's footrest again, and I grit my teeth and clenched my jaw to force myself to avoid spitting at him to knock it off and grow up.

"Please! Please! Please! **Please! Please! Meredith,** **please! Meredith! Meredith! Meredith!"**.

Again, the more I ignored him, the louder he got, and I worried that we might wind up with police at the door after a neighbor called in a noise disturbance since it was well after quiet hours for both the complex and the city. Even so, I knew I couldn't acknowledge him no matter how long this went on. He kicked the footrest again, this time stumbling backward a bit and almost losing his balance. I don't know if this was what finally made him stop, but as I turned my head, sunk my teeth into my lower lip, and held my breath, he backed away from the chair and threw a hand up.

"Fine! Be selfish. I'll figure something else out!".

He stormed past me, making sure he pushed the chair with his hip as he passed, swiping his lighter off the counter (for what reason, I don't know since he claimed he had no cigarettes) and stomping out the door, making sure to slam it behind him. It didn't take long to realize he hadn't gone far, as he began talking out loud from the deck about what a bitch I was and how "all he was asking for" was a pack of cigarettes, so "What was the big deal because she owes me anyway?"

Eventually, things went quiet, and I guess he chose not to wake me up when he came back from wherever he went. I quickly reached down and pulled my wallet from my purse, tucking it underneath me, and I remember falling asleep being thankful that what had happened hadn't ended with police intervention, though in hindsight, maybe it wouldn't have been such a terrible thing if it had.

I had done it! I had set a boundary with him…. *and kept it!*

You might be thinking, *"So you set a boundary. Is it that big a deal?"*

Yes! As a recovering codependent, it really was because it was a pivotal turning point. This was the first time I had ever been able to tell him no and stand by it no matter how relentlessly he tried to change my mind. Normally the guilt would be enough to make me give in to whatever it was he was asking for, and I'd kick myself later. Guilt? Why would I feel guilty for telling someone no? Remember I said that this is an earmark of codependency. We feel as though caretaking is what we were put on this earth to do, even if what we're doing really isn't taking care of someone (Such as was the case with my tendency to give in when he would beg me to buy him cigarettes because he had spent his last $10 on vodka. Sounds more like enabling, doesn't it?! Exactly.). Telling someone else no feels to us like we're doing something wrong or bad because we're putting ourselves first, and who the hell are we to do *that*, after all?!

So, *boundaries*. What is this *boundaries* thing? This is such a foreign and difficult concept for those entangled in a relationship with an addict. Think of the parent who can't say "no" to their adult child after being arrested for the use of their substance and calls for bail money, or the friend who loans an addict money because they feel bad after the addict tells them that they have no food. Boundaries stretch across the full breadth of relationship situations, though of course certainly sharply prevalent in romantic relationships in particular. Simply put, boundaries are how we define who we are and what we will and won't accept from others to feel safe and respected in a personal relationship. Think of them as a personal property line of sorts, that "line in the sand." We tell people what and where the lines are with the expectation that the other person will respect them. In healthy relationships, they are. This, however, is not and typically cannot be the case when talking about relationships with people who struggle with addiction. This becomes even more true when you throw codependency into the mix.

I feel like I need to stop briefly and clarify something. I've been using the terms "healthy" and "unhealthy" a lot throughout this book, and I want to make sure I am crystal clear about what I mean. I am by NO means saying or suggesting that people who suffer from codependency or addiction are disturbed, dangerous, or crazy. *Unhealthy* is exactly that, regardless of the form it takes — as much as having a cold, the flu, or pneumonia. With the proper care and resources, recovery is 100% possible. This is no less true for both addiction and codependency. The difference here is that addiction and codependency are as much emotional illnesses as physical and sometimes more so. While a cold can be killed with rest and medication, addiction and codependency take far more comprehensive and multifaceted approaches to effectively bring about and maintain recovery because of the mental/emotional element. Use and abuse of substances usually happen because the addict is trying to escape from the pain that they are too afraid to confront themselves (Keep in mind I said *usually*. I know that not everyone abuses drugs or alcohol from an emotional place. I'm just saying that more often than not, this is the case, even if it doesn't appear to be from the outside). Fear is an emotion. Codependents are drawn into toxic relationships because of deep *feelings* of insecurity and inferiority that cause them only to be able to find any sense of self-worth if they are putting others first. While any physical impacts of either condition can certainly be addressed, if the emotional wounds are left untreated, the codependent will likely continue to repeat the same behaviors until those emotions are directly and proactively faced. Addicts and codependents aren't crazy. They're hurting, and like anyone with a wound, they're trying to find any way they can to get the bleeding to stop so the wound can heal. For addicts, that's their chosen substance. For codependents, it's caretaking and putting everyone else first, whether toxic or not. Neither set out to hurt others. They're just trying to make their own pain stop.

Back to boundaries. I've gone into a lot of detail about codependency's impacts, and boundaries are a major part of it. Understanding the causes of codependency and how the codependent feels about themselves, it shouldn't be too much of a surprise that boundaries are difficult for them. The person who feels no self-worth is also not going to feel that they have any right or reason to tell someone else no. They feel worthless. How can a worthless person tell someone else, no? This is an excruciatingly painful part of the codependent wound. People with addictions also struggle with boundaries because they are driven to fulfill that need I spoke of earlier at any cost. That can and does often include disregarding others' boundaries. Now put this combination together. Consider why and how a codependent would be drawn to someone with an addiction and have difficulty recognizing the relationship as unhealthy and then setting and maintaining boundaries once the relationship is established. The addict with the need plus the codependent whose need is to take care of others with unmet needs equals an ever-escalating cycle of manipulation, one-sidedness, fear, and toxicity. Neither are good with boundaries — the codependent with setting them, and the addict with respecting them.

This leads to the question of what boundaries can look like. This is a question with a wide breadth of answers because boundaries are as personal to the individual as the codependent wound itself. What is acceptable for one person may be utterly intolerable for another, and naturally, each relationship is different, so the lines within each relationship are also different.

Consider this example:

A mother has a son in his 40s who has struggled with alcohol addiction for most of his life. As a result, he has also had considerable difficulty maintaining his own housing and holding down a job because he never has any money. The mother is more than ten years sober and takes her sobriety very seriously. She knows that if she lets her son stay with her, he will drink, so when he calls from a homeless shelter and asks if he can stay with her for a while, she tells him this is not something she can allow. He begs, telling her that he has nowhere to go and will

*have to sleep on the street, and it hurts her heart to turn her son
away, but she tells him again that he cannot stay with her.*

The first response to this from many people might be,
"She's his mother. She should do what she can to help him." No.
His mother drew a boundary. Is it her responsibility to make sure
that her adult son has a roof over his head? She knew that she
had to protect her own sobriety, so she did what she had to do to
ensure that her personal lines were not risked by letting someone
come into her home whom she knew would likely end up drinking.
That's a boundary. It doesn't mean she doesn't care or love him.
Of course, she does.

Boundaries are not easy to draw, especially for someone
who experiences so much self-doubt in their own worth, to begin
with. For the codependent with this inner war waging inside them,
telling someone else no for their own sake is tantamount to
stapling a huge, flashing neon "SELFISH" sign onto their
forehead for the world to see. They experience such an
overwhelming sense of guilt at the thought of turning someone
else away to put themselves first that they would rather take on
the consequences of saying yes to whatever it is even though
they probably don't want to, just to make that terrible guilty ache
go away.

I can speak to this personally. The situation I opened this
chapter with was by far neither the first nor the last time he came
to me to buy him cigarettes because he was out of money. The
addict, knowing this goes after that vulnerability because they
recognize the high likelihood that it'll ultimately get them whatever
it is they want, often using words like "favor" and "help" the way
my ex did to soften that wound enough to pry it open. Explaining
it this way makes addicts sound like predators; they're not. What
they are, though, is unable to take care of themselves. They're so
enmeshed in their addiction, and the cycle of repercussions that
come with that addiction that they can't see beyond it to figure out
how to get themselves off the cycle and back on their feet, so for
them, someone else's personal boundaries are often seen as little
more than a hurdle to be jumped to get to their goal at the time.
Even more, this is the case with the codependent because it
takes so much less poking and prodding than it would someone
with secure self-worth and strong, confident boundaries for what
they will and won't tolerate from others. The codependent sees
the chance to do something for someone in need, even if what
the addict wants isn't an actual need. Like with him. He
didn't *need* cigarettes. He wouldn't have died having to go a night
without them. He *wanted* them, and because he was drunk, that
was all he cared about. In his mind, I should have been happy to

do it for him because he framed it as being a "solid" — his favorite word for a favor, which he knew was an emotional soft spot for me. This is why I had to say "no" 87 times, even as he kept pushing. Honestly, I'm amazed he actually gave up. That was a first.

So, what else can a boundary look like?

- Refusing to bail a loved one out of jail after an arrest related to their addiction.

- Refusing to give the addict money.

- Not helping the addict pay their bills.

- Not giving the addict a place to stay or telling them what will and will not be tolerated if you do give them a place to stay, and what will happen if they cross those lines, and then following through on those repercussions! Follow through is such a crucial part of setting and maintaining boundaries. Not following through tells the addict that the boundaries are essentially hollow, and you'll let them get away with breaking them — and they will!).

- Not driving the addict around, or even giving them gas money. Never, ever give an addict still active in their addiction money!

- Not taking care of responsibilities for the addict that they should be taking care of themselves.

- Not making excuses for or defending the addict when they engage in poor behavior.

- Not buying things for the addict. For example, when he broke his phone, my immediate instinct was to get him a new one. I didn't, but I had to talk myself out of it, because that would only enable him down the road).

This is just the tip of the boundary-drawing iceberg. There are many, many ways to draw and enforce boundaries. It comes down to what you need to feel safe and comfortable in your world and with the people in it. If a choice or behavior is not acceptable to you, don't accept it. You can't control others, but you can make choices for yourself to ensure that those you allow in your life respect your right to live comfortably. I know that this is so much easier said than done, but even starting with smaller boundaries here and there will help build that feeling of self-empowerment. The more you do it, the easier it becomes. When I first started drawing boundaries with him, it always caused me tremendous guilt from that terrible feeling of not being enough and therefore having no right to speak up for myself — but I DO have that right, and so do you! The addict's decisions are theirs, but that doesn't mean you have to accept them in your world. This is such a difficult concept for codependents to understand, but with time and practice, that terrible "lesson" we were taught that left us believing we're not enough can and will be reversed. Don't get me wrong – I still sometimes have a hard time setting boundaries. It doesn't just suddenly become like breathing. I have to be mindful every day to ensure that that wound that I'm working on healing doesn't get the better of me and goad me into doing something unhealthy, and of course, there are those in my life whom I have a harder time drawing boundaries with, but that's okay. One boundary at a time is all we can do.

Let's look at one more aspect of boundary-setting, the part that so many of us fear: The response.

It's damned near inevitable that when you set a boundary with someone, chances are they may not like it. Addicts, in particular, are infamous for referring to boundaries we set as "rules" and are quick to cry that we are trying to "control them". God knows I heard this accusation constantly, and at first, I immediately backed down, believing he was right. I realized, though, that *true* boundary setting is, as I mentioned earlier, not about trying to control the behaviors of others because we have neither the power nor the right to do that. True boundary setting is about asserting our right to speak for ourselves in terms of what we are and are not okay with accepting in our lives so that we can live comfortably, contentedly, and safely. Nevertheless, we still often feel intimidated by the idea of speaking up for ourselves because we fear how the other person might respond. This is especially true when setting boundaries with an addict. Let me stop here and say that if you're in a relationship with someone violent, **the** most important thing is always your safety. If you feel like not setting boundaries will keep you safer, I absolutely encourage you to find other ways to protect yourself. I don't want anyone putting themselves into a situation that could cause them harm. This is even more true if the situation involves children, as they cannot protect themselves. Please always keep safety first and foremost in your mind when dealing with an addict.

So, if violence isn't a risk of setting boundaries with your addicted loved one, what kinds of reactions might you expect, and how can you respond?

There is a high likelihood that your addicted loved one will react with anger. They may tell you that you're being controlling or manipulative. They may try to throw past demons they know about you in your face or use their own past against you to try and make you feel guilty. "How can you treat me like this?! You know that's what my mom/dad used to do to me!" or "I'm not your mom. I'm not trying to control you. You don't have to be so defensive." He was notorious for this one. It was always my mom. "I'm not your mom. I'm not your dad". He always threw this one at me when I set boundaries with him. It seldom made sense when he did, but I knew he was just trying to project to deflect. Granted, I didn't know that at first, so my instant reaction was anger right back –- but this never helped. It only escalated him further. It was when I *stopped* responding that he started to back off. Instead of firing back, I calmly responded with, "I can't control what you do, but I can control what I accept as okay in my own world, and that's what I'm doing.". It became obvious that he didn't know how to respond to that, so his only recourse was to back off.

I acknowledge, of course, that this isn't always possible, nor will it always work, but the more calmly you're able to respond when someone reacts to a boundary you've set with anger, the better able you'll be to diffuse the situation and maintain that boundary whether through their acceptance of it or their choice to take the consequences of not doing so. I used to give him a choice: "You can either stay here and be sober or go somewhere else and drink, but if I find alcohol here, you won't be allowed to stay.". At first, it was difficult for *me* to adhere to that because of the guilt I felt, but I realized that every time I set that boundary then didn't follow through, I was inviting him to disrespect me all over again. As hard as it was, I knew I had to actually make sure that if I told him, he'd need to leave if I found he was drinking that I made him do it. The more I did that, the more he realized that he wasn't going to get away with trying to get around my boundaries. He'd scoff. He'd complain. He'd beg. He'd try to deflect. The less this worked, though, the more I saw he started *choosing* to go somewhere else rather than try to change my mind. The consequence of follow-through is absolutely critical to the success of a boundary.

I know that putting it that way probably sounds a bit daunting, but it doesn't have to be. Start small. "No, I won't drive you to..." or "No, I can't do ... right now". Get yourself comfortable with the word "no" because that's half the battle right there. I started by telling him I wouldn't give him money for cigarettes and *sticking to it.* The more I did this, the easier it became and the less guilty I felt, until one day I heard myself saying, "I can't let you stay here if you're going to drink.". I shocked myself. I shocked *him.* Again, I was starting at the beginning, and at first, I'd buckle to "please sweetie. I'm sorry." And "I have nowhere else to go.". From there, it became that he was going to hotels, but *I* was paying for it because I didn't want him to be on the street. I had set a boundary, but I was still allowing his choices to impact *me.* I was making his shelter my problem, and not even just my problem –- my *responsibility.* Then I began insisting that he use whatever money he did have to cover his own rooms. I knew it was working because suddenly, I was repeatedly accused of "changing.". "Sweetie, you've changed.". He didn't like that I was setting a boundary because it was making his life more uncomfortable.

I remember once during a heated discussion I was having with him in which I finally challenged him, asking him what he wanted from me. He replied with, "Sweetie, I want you.". Without even thinking about it, I fired back with, "No. You want me without boundaries". His response?

"True."

There it was. He wanted the relationship but on *his* terms.

An addict may also respond to your boundary-setting by trying to give you an ultimatum. "If that's what you're going to do, then fine. I'll leave you." To a codependent, this is the worst threat there is — abandonment. Almost every codependent fears abandonment, because to some degree, that's where and how the initial codependent wound was born in the first place. Now, here is this person that we've essentially devoted ourselves to, and they're threatening to abandon us if we don't do what they want. It's manipulation. I can almost 100% assure you that it's also all talk. The goal is to control. That should be the motto of the active addict –- *the goal is to control.* As long as they can maintain control and a consistent supply of their needed substance or behavior, they're fine.

At the same time, if they're willing to walk away because you won't give in to what they want even though they know it would make you uncomfortable, how much do they really care about you? Someone who loves you won't ask you to do something that makes you uncomfortable just to make them happy. Ultimatums are a favorite tool of the addict because they can be an immediate way to get what they want. If they threaten you with something they know you don't want to happen, you're more likely to give in. This is where it becomes crucial to stick to your boundary because this is where they're testing you. It's tough to do, but the addict is less likely to try and manipulate you if they know you're going to stand firm in the boundaries you set. It's also important, particularly in this context, to clearly understand the difference between an ultimatum/threat and a boundary. The active addict will try to spin a boundary you set off as giving them an ultimatum, and the two are not the same. An ultimatum is a restriction placed on *someone else* with the threat of an unpleasant outcome if the behavior or decision demanded isn't complied to. As we've already discussed, a boundary is a line drawn for *yourself* that tells others how you will and will not let yourself be treated. One makes a demand of someone else. The other asserts your own right to be comfortable and feel safe in your own world. There's a clearly decided difference. They will try to twist one into the other. Don't let them confuse you. Doing what's best for you is not the same as making a demand of someone else.

An addict may give you the silent treatment if you stand firm in your boundary. You know what? Honestly, the best thing you can do in this case is to take it as a blessing. While it may be uncomfortable and even upsetting, the silent treatment is far less stressful than the addict who keeps coming at you and coming at you to try and change your mind. It's also far more respectful. The silent treatment is their way of masking giving up as anger — an emotion they know will likely make you even more uncomfortable. If they're going to give up, they're damned sure going to try to make you feel bad about it in the process. Don't. It's their problem, and they'll get over it. Trust me. They'll find another source to go to for whatever it is they couldn't get from you. In the beginning, when he used to stop talking to me after I refused him something, it was unsettling. It didn't take me long, however, to appreciate the gift for what it was. No arguing. No coaxing. No guilt. No anger. Just... silence. Eventually, he got over it. They always do. Either way, it's not your responsibility.

Unfortunately, boundaries often wind up not being limited to use with your addicted loved one. You may find that you need to set them with others in their lives as well. If it's your partner, you may find that you need to set firm boundaries with his family members or friends who may try to manipulate you. Even the best of intentions are essentially manipulative if you've made your boundaries clear with your addicted loved ones, and then family and friends get involved on their behalf. In the world of narcissistic abuse, these are called flying monkeys, and it's appropriate in this case, too. These are the people who "swoop in" and try to advocate, defend, speak up for or otherwise manipulate you into continuing to enable the addict. The intention may not be manipulation. That has certainly been the case with his mother. She had reached out to me a handful of times requesting various things to help him, even though she was forthright in telling me before I left that I needed to cut him off and let him figure things out for himself. I've come to know her over the years. She doesn't have a dishonest or manipulative bone in her body... but she's also his mother. She's going to prioritize him, naturally. Even though she strongly encouraged me to walk away, she still comes to me when she needs something for him, whether it's to check his email for something or even file paperwork for him for things he needs. I know she's not *trying* to manipulate me because that's not who she is, but it's still manipulation, especially since she was so emphatic about my need to cut all ties and move on.

How can I do that if I'm still being asked to do things for him? How can I do that if I'm still being told of the terrible condition he's in? This can happen in any relationship. If you have an addicted family member, you may get other family members coming to you trying to speak up for them and telling you that you "should" help them as family. If it's a friendship relationship, you may find yourself caught between the addict and another friend trying to play peacemaker by nudging you to be more supportive.

The addict may even *send* others in to try and manipulate you into doing what they want. They are not above crying stories to others to try and paint loved ones as terrible people who are treating them poorly to garner enough empathy to then nudge them into coming at you on their behalf. As previously discussed, active addicts are master manipulators. They can spin any situation into a self-pity story, and in the continued effort to protect their secret, they have no problem doing so.

Just as with your addicted loved one, you need to stand your ground with those they recruit on their behalf, as well. They may not mean any harm to you by speaking up for the addict, but it's still harmful. Don't feel guilty about establishing boundaries with them. There's no reason for anyone else to become involved in your relationship, and it's your right to stand firm in not allowing them to, no matter what their intentions may be. If they feel that the addicted loved one needs to or should be helped, let them do it. It's important for your own emotional well-being that you maintain boundaries. It's perfectly acceptable for you to tell someone trying to involve themselves in your relationship with your addicted loved one that you're not comfortable with them putting themselves in the middle and that you're doing what you feel is best. They don't need any further explanation.

Boundaries are a tricky road to navigate as it is, and they become even more challenging when dealing with an addict. Everything in our nature compels us to "help" them, and it's difficult to understand that most of the time, we're not actually helping them at all. As codependents, it's even harder because we feel as though we're going against who we are and, more importantly, who we think we should be if we don't step in and "rescue" in whatever form it may be taking at the time. After all, we're *supposed* to take care of everyone else because that's where our own worth is found, right? This is the single most important belief that we need to heal and to begin drawing healthy relationships into our lives finally.

That begins with boundaries.

April 2020.

"It's not mine."

I stared at him, slack-jawed, my fist clenching the half-empty bottle of vodka so tightly that my hand was shaking from the pressure. I had gotten up to kick a toy that the cat had managed to lose under the recliner out and instead kicked out the bottle. Was he *seriously* trying to convince me that he hadn't sneaked it into the house yet again? Even after four years, he was still lying to me and thinking I'd believe him?

"Not YOURS? Who the hell else's would it be?! Are you going to tell me it's the cat's?!"

I could feel the rage surging and churning into nausea in the pit of my stomach and boiling up into my throat. I had to look away from him and take a deep breath to keep from vomiting right there in front of him.

"You probably decided you wanted to drink, and you knew you could blame me for it."

It was like having my feet kicked out from under me, and for a split second, I was so stunned that I didn't know whether to scream or laugh. He had come up with some out-there excuses to try and explain why he had yet again broken the boundary he had agreed to, but this was a first. I opened my mouth, and then I closed it as if I had suddenly forgotten how to talk. Taking a deep breath, I chucked the bottle into the kitchen sink, turned back to face him, and I could feel the grin pulling at the sides of my mouth.

*"You're **kidding**. Are you really trying to turn this around on me?! I have to hand it to you – THAT was a good one!"*

We both knew I didn't drink. We both knew he was the only one in the house who did. He knew I knew it was his bottle, but hell if he wasn't still going to try and get me to believe I was wrong! He huffed and turned from me, flopping down on the bed.

"It's not mine. I don't know whose it is, but it's not mine".

I debated whether or not to include a chapter on gaslighting. Typically, gaslighting is seen as a primary factor in relationships with narcissists, but it's also prevalent in relationships with addicts, not for the same reasons but present just the same. Regardless of the context it's used in it's cruel, and I think it's important to explore it further so that if you recognize any of what is discussed in this chapter in your own relationship, you can take what you feel would be the most appropriate measures to address it.

Gaslighting.

Coined from a 1930's play made into a movie, gaslighting is the intentional act of trying to make a person question their reality. The premise of the plot was a husband who was intentionally trying to make his wife feel crazy by making subtle changes around their home (such as dimming the light in a room) and then asking her if she noticed or did it, bringing her to start questioning herself more and more. If you question your reality, you question yourself, and if you question yourself, you're more likely to believe that you were the one who was wrong.

Gaslighting is an insidious form of manipulation because it's destabilizing and can often be and often is covert. Think about it – if you're constantly questioning yourself, how much energy or focus are you likely to have left even to realize you're being manipulated, let alone respond to it? What makes gaslighting even worse is that like with boundaries, there are endless forms it can take. He knew damn well that the pint of vodka wasn't mine. That didn't stop him from trying to get me to question myself to the point where I wondered if maybe he was right and I was blaming him for something he didn't do, despite that there was literally no other conceivable way it even could have gotten into the house.

*"You just **want** to find something to blame me for. You want to find something to get angry at me for"*

This was another one he often used on me. *I* was the manipulative one. *I* was the one causing the problem. He often used my past experience with my first alcoholic ex to suggest that the problem wasn't that he drank but that *I* had a problem with drinking in general. Again –- he wasn't the problem -- I was. It becomes easy to see how gaslighting can be so destabilizing. We begin to feel like we're crazy, and that's the goal of the gaslighter. Gaslighting is not restricted to romantic relationships either. Not by any means. Parents and children (and vice versa), siblings, friends, co-workers, and supervisors (and vice versa) — these are all relationships in which gaslighting can and often does happen. When addiction is thrown into the mix, it becomes damn near inevitable. I mentioned that gaslighting can take on a multitude of forms. Let's take a look at some of them:

- They tell obvious lies. They know it's a lie. They know *we* know it's a lie, but they're still going to try and convince us because, at this point, you're not sure if anything they say is true. It keeps you constantly unbalanced.

- They say or do something, then deny it when called on it. They are intentionally trying to destabilize you to make you question your sanity.

- They tell you how loveable you'd be if only you didn't have negative traits. Those traits could be emotional or physical. "If only you weren't so sensitive, you'd be easier to like," or "Imagine how pretty you'd be if you wore makeup." My paternal relatives were pros at this when I was a kid, telling me how loveable and pretty I'd be if I was thinner. It's a terrible, vicious, heartless way to treat anyone.

- They praise you. You might be saying, "Wait... praise? Isn't that a good thing?". Normally, yes, but not when being used as a gaslighting technique because, in this form, it's used to keep you hoovered in. Here is this person who is constantly insulting you, belittling you, devaluing you, and mistreating you, and suddenly they're telling you they love you, and how wonderful you are.

- They project. This is another huge gaslighting behavior. The addict will project their poor behavior onto you. He constantly accused me of cheating on him, yet I came to find out at the end that he was the one being, in the very least emotionally unfaithful, telling other women he loved and wanted to be with them. Projection is a tool of the guilty conscience. They know you're not doing what they're accusing you of, but to get the spotlight off of them, they'll say you're actually the one engaging in whatever the behavior is.

- They try to turn people against you. Again, this is such a horribly destabilizing form of manipulation because not only are they trying to manipulate you, but now they're dragging other people into it to try and gang up on you as well. Often they will tell other people that you're doing terrible things or treating them poorly to gain sympathy, in turn making them look like the victim. He was telling people that I kicked him out on the street once I got my college degree because I decided he wasn't smart enough for me — I got my degree three years before I even met him, and he knew it. The fact that I finished college was always a source of insecurity for him. I knew it made him feel inferior for some reason, though I never knew why, and I never once used it against him in any way. I never gave him any reason to think that I believed myself to be smarter than he was, let alone used it as a reason to kick him out. He knew that too, but it didn't stop him from using it as a reason to cry to others and get sympathy.

- They insist that everyone else is lying about them. Their ex. Their mother. Their friends. Everyone is out to get them. Everyone is out to turn you against them and tell lies about them to do that. At the beginning of the relationship, he used to refer to his ex-wife as a psychopath who told their daughter lies about him. Later I came to find out that he was telling other people lies about me, too.

It's easy to see why gaslighting is so terrible. While the addict's own insecurity drives these behaviors, it comes off as an attack on the loved one, regardless of the form it takes. For the codependent, that destabilizing feeling is utterly dehumanizing. We struggle with those feelings of not being enough as it is, so behaviors aimed at us that are deliberately intended to make us doubt ourselves even further can really leave us feeling small and worthless.

How do we know we're being gaslighted? That can be a tough question to answer, but there are ways to tell.

- You begin questioning if you really are too sensitive or even crazy.
- You often feel confused and unstable.

- You constantly apologize, even if you're not sure what you're apologizing for, just to keep the peace.

- You often make excuses for your loved one's behaviors. You know deep down that the behavior isn't okay, but you're quick to jump to their defense and cover for them with others.

- You constantly second-guess yourself and your decisions, feeling like you can't do anything right without someone else validating that it's right.

- You know something is wrong, but you can't put a finger on what it is. You just know that something feels off.

- You find yourself questioning even more if you're good enough, pretty enough, smart enough –– enough in general. You feel essentially validated in that feeling that you're not.

Couldn't these also be symptoms of depression or anxiety? Absolutely. The difference is that with gaslighting, a second person is involved who is deliberately trying to make you feel this way. Anxiety and depression are hard enough, but for the person struggling with codependency to have someone else, let alone someone they trusted to love and care about them purposely trying to make them question themselves is the ultimate betrayal, both painful and dehumanizing. We try so hard to be there; to help them, take care of them, and support them, only to have them try to confuse and demean us in the most insidious ways; using our struggles with self-worth against us for their own gain and benefit.

The next question you might be asking is, what are some things a gaslighter might say?

- "You're so sensitive/you're overreacting. Why do you take everything so personally?"

- "You just misunderstood me." (Use of "just" in this context is used to blame and intended to minimize the person's feelings and reactions as wrong or trivial.)

- "I was only joking. Can't you take a joke?"

- "That's not what I said/You're just imaging/making things up." (Again, with the word "just" as a minimizer.)

- "You see something that isn't there. You need help."

- "No one believes you anyway" (Talk about devaluation!).

- "You love to try and blame things on me when it's really you."

- "You're the problem, not me."

- "Why do you keep bringing up the past? Just let it go."

- "I wouldn't have said/done that if you hadn't provoked me."
  (I did something bad, but it was *your* fault.)

Pretty terrible, isn't it? So how can we even begin to respond to such behavior? In a perfect situation, we would just ignore it, but unfortunately, it's not nearly that simple, especially with addiction and codependency. It's important to remember gaslighting for what it is: manipulation. No matter what they say, this is not about you. In the beginning, I absorbed SO much of what he said to me — calling me sensitive and crazy, yelling and screaming at me about how I always blame others but never take any accountability myself, and how if I didn't like being yelled at I shouldn't give him a reason to. I already battled feelings of low self-worth, and now here he was telling me that all the things I thought about myself were true, except that they weren't. He was yelling and screaming at me, calling me names, and I was reacting emotionally, yet I was "too sensitive."

In what world does that make sense? In the world of the addict, that's where. Any normal person would be hurt if someone they thought loved them was verbally assaulting them and would be well within their right to express that hurt. Remember, though, that the addict is not only under the influence of a behavior-altering substance but is also coming from a place of deep worthlessness themselves, so of course, they're going to project. It's easier to throw your insecurities at someone else than face them head-on. It may not be right, it may not be fair, but it's easier. It's easier to project than it is to reflect. With this being the case, back to the question of how you can respond to being gaslighted:

- Make sure it really is gaslighting. A difference of opinion is not gaslighting. Arguing is not gaslighting. Gaslighting is a continuing pattern of manipulation. The person doesn't merely disagree with you. They're flat out calling you crazy and over-sensitive, trying to make you doubt yourself. If it doesn't feel right, if it doesn't feel healthy, then it probably isn't. Trust your instinct.

- If you can separate from it, do so. Move to a different room. Leave completely. Find some way to get some distance so that you can clear your head and regain perspective. Remaining calm is crucial to effectively combatting gaslighting. Giving in to emotion — anger, hurt, sadness, frustration — and letting the gaslighter see the emotion gives them further ammunition. It's not worth it. Find a person with whom or a place where you can blow off that steam safely. I know that this is easier said than done, but don't let the gaslighter pull it out of you. That's what they want; your reaction, so they can play off it and gaslight you even more.

- Hold confidence in what you know to be true. Now that we've gone into detail about gaslighting and what it's intended to do, you know that the entire purpose of it is to make you doubt and question yourself even though deep down you know that what you experienced is the truth. Don't let the gaslighter convince you otherwise. Their whole objective is to throw you off-kilter in the hopes of deflecting attention from themselves so that they can continue to use. You know the truth. Trust it. Trust yourself. This is the first step back from being gaslighted.

- While documenting the attempts in ways such as recording conversations and writing things down is an option, I recommend doing this solely for your own peace of mind. Please do NOT do so with the expectation that it will somehow make the gaslighter realize what they're doing and stop. They're well aware of what they're doing, and no matter how much proof you throw at them, they will continue to deny and deflect. Don't exacerbate the madness. If you're going to document, do it for yourself.

- Self-care, self-care, self-care. SO important. The more you begin to take care of yourself, the stronger you become in standing solidly in what you will and will not accept from the people in your life. The more I focused on doing things that I knew were healthy for myself –– eating healthy, journaling, trying to get enough sleep, talking to and spending time with the healthy positive people in my life the better and better I started getting at feeling confident in the boundaries I was setting with him, knowing that it wasn't about controlling him but taking care of myself emotionally. I had no reason to apologize or feel guilty for that, no matter how he tried to make me feel otherwise.

Of course, the addict will try to dissuade, discourage, and diminish your efforts. Remember, this is about maintaining control so that their ability to continue using isn't put at risk. The person who recognizes their behaviors for what they are and calls them out on them poses a direct threat to that control. Therefore, the addict will say and do whatever they believe might work to ensure that the threat doesn't become a reality. They make it about you, but it's not. They make it about you because they are too afraid to focus on themselves. It's not easy to hold ground when you're being gaslighted, but the stronger you're able to become in doing so, the less power the gaslighter will hold in being able to manipulate you.

Abuse is never okay!

Much like the chapter on gaslighting, I went back and forth with myself on whether or not to include a chapter on abuse. I don't want to suggest that all addicts are abusive or that abuse should *ever* be an expected part of a relationship. Unlike past chapters in which I opened them with an example from my own relationship, I decided against doing that with this chapter because my goal is not to throw him under the bus and make him look like a monster. I think it's important to further explore the various forms of abuse so that if you recognize any in your own relationship, you can hopefully begin to take the necessary steps to get away, get safe, and start healing.

Generally, there are understood to be five types of abuse:

- Emotional
- Physical
- Mental
- Sexual
- Financial

Some would say that mental and emotional abuse are the same. While that remains a matter of personal opinion, I think it's safe to say that the wounds of emotional/mental abuse are far more insidious than those of physical abuse because they impact the victim from the inside, and therefore are far harder and take far longer to heal. Unfortunately, abuse happens frequently in relationships in which one of the individuals involved is an addict. As discussed in an earlier chapter, these substances alter the brain's chemical messengers, often causing drastic, blatantly noticeable, and often negative behavior changes. The substance exacerbates anger, resentment, rage, jealousy, and above all, insecurity — all of these feelings and emotions are essentially encouraged to come out. Since the addict's inhibitions are also lowered due to the changes in the brain's emotional center, they become far more likely to allow them out than they would when they are sober.

As with gaslighting, abuse can take on many forms, from yelling and screaming to name-calling to outright physical violence and even rape. Manipulation is also a form of abuse, but because it is often so covert in its presentation, it's typically left off the list when discussing abuse. Make no mistake – because of the intention of harm behind manipulation, it *is* abuse. This kind of abuse is considered the most common form in relationships with narcissists because it's the primary tool they use for maintaining control of the victim. Gaslighting, projecting, deflecting, devaluing — all of these are tools of the narcissist. Again, that's not to say that all addicts are narcissists, but there does seem to be a connection between narcissism and substance use. For this book, though, I will focus on the "typical" forms of abuse, as they are far broader and more varied.

Starting with the obvious one: Physical abuse. This encompasses sexual abuse as well, though certainly sexual abuse is and should be its own category. What can/does physical abuse look like?

- Hitting
- Punching
- Kicking
- Slapping
- Grabbing
- Gripping/Physical control
- Scratching/biting
- Hair pulling

These are the obvious ones, but frighteningly, physical abuse is not limited to the obvious. If you think about the different ways the physical body can be injured, it can really run a chill up the spine. Turn on the news at any given time, and you're bound to hear a story about someone being arrested for choking their partner, or stabbing or shooting their parents, even drowning their own child. The human body is sensitive and vulnerable, starting with the skin, which is a living being in itself and protects the even more fragile workings of the inner system. This is why physical violence is the most immediately dangerous form of abuse there is. Not only does it expose the body to highly injurious treatment, but it can and often does quickly escalate and become more frequent. This is why I have emphasized and will continue to emphasize the importance of safety as the primary priority when there is violence in a relationship. We want so much to believe that if we keep trying, it will get better. *It won't.* While it's critical that if you're being physically abused, you get away, the most dangerous time for an abuse victim is typically right after they've left their abuser. Remember also that substance use altars behavior, more often than not escalating instability, aggression, and volatility. This makes for an extremely treacherous mix for the loved one who is planning an escape. Please always ensure that your safety is being kept at the forefront of any plans you might be making to leave, even more so if there are children involved. The violent addict who sees that they are losing that control that they grip so tightly won't hesitate to heighten the violence to ensure that you don't leave and take that power from them. Some will even kill to hold on to it. I don't say it to cause fear, but this is not the subject to withhold facts and the truth about.

Emotional/mental abuse is far more devious because physical abuse injures the outside, and emotional abuse wounds the inside. That's not to say that physical abuse doesn't cause emotional damage because it absolutely does, but emotional abuse is deliberately and cunningly aimed at the feelings and self-worth of the victim. Name-calling, devaluing, belittling, insulting, etc. It all takes a terrible and detrimental toll on the emotions and breaks the victim down, which is the purpose. The broken-down loved one won't fight or in any other way threaten the addict's delicate grip on their secret, let alone even *think* about leaving. The true insidiousness of emotional abuse is that after hearing it enough, we begin to believe that the things they're saying to us and about us are true. It may seem like name-calling or insults should be easy to ignore, but it doesn't work that way — especially when it's constant, and even more especially so if the victim is a codependent. They already come from a place of such damaged self-worth that someone they care about and whom they believe cares about them telling them they're worthless, stupid, ugly, etc. is enough to eradicate their sense of self and convince them that they deserve the way they're being treated because they're not worth anything better.

An angry addict flinging insults and devaluing the codependent will have to put minimal effort into being effective. Ugly, stupid, fat, crazy, worthless, useless — imagine the damage these words can have on a person who already believed they were these things before the addict came into the picture. It doesn't even stop there, though. This kind of abuse can be viciously covert, disguised as a " suggestion," " constructive criticism," or even what amounts to a backhanded compliment. My family members used to do this to me all the time when I was younger, " You'd be so much prettier if you'd just lose some weight." Were they calling me pretty? It may sound like it, framed by "so much prettie*r*," but no. This was a backhanded compliment of the worst kind because if I reacted to it, I was further attacked for being "too sensitive" (Gaslighting! See? It can happen in any relationship!)

The same things happen in emotionally abusive relationships. It doesn't have to be an outright name or insult to be abusive. Telling someone they would be something positive *if* they changed something about themselves is devaluing and abusive. Attacking a physical trait or perceived " weakness" about someone is abusive. "Why can't you be more like...." is abusive. Using someone's past experiences and traumas against them is absolutely abusive. He used to use my first abusive relationship against me when he got drunk, telling me he could "understand" why my first alcoholic ex used to push me around. I started wondering if maybe he was right. Maybe I *was* that difficult to deal with. I wasn't, of course, but he had to turn it around on me to relieve himself of responsibility and break me down so that I wouldn't fight him. That is the disgusting nature of emotional abuse. There were things that he said to me that hurt me so much more deeply than any physical act he could've carried out against me ever would have. They still sting months and years later because it was deliberate emotional cruelty using my insecurities against me from someone who claimed to love me. While I'm in no way meaning to minimize the severity of physical abuse, the wounds of emotional abuse often take so much longer to heal because of how internalized they become. For someone who struggles with codependency, these internal wounds not only take a long time to heal, but they also compound the wound that was already there, making it that much more relentlessly and unforgivingly painful.

Sexual abuse is horrible, no matter what form it takes. Molestation, sexual assault, rape. It's all inexcusable. *Any* unwanted sexual advance is also abuse; sexual remarks, comments about someone's body, propositions, unwanted touch, even unwelcomed flirting. Again, remember this can become even more of an issue with an addict because of their lowered inhibitions and inability to regulate their emotions. He was *all* about sex when he was drunk and was also very persistent. He was convinced that I wanted it even though I was saying I didn't. In the beginning, it was difficult for me to tell him no because I was still so strongly attracted and attached to him. The intimacy between us equated to love, and I craved it. As time went on, and I realized that the majority of our intimate times together happened when he was drinking, it started to feel more like he needed to be drunk to be intimate with me, and the pain of that was enough to turn me off to intimacy with him. Even with my codependency, I needed to feel that emotional intimacy from an honest place in order to want to be physically intimate, and it hurt to think that he had to be drunk to want to be with me. Towards the end of the relationship, he pushed hard to try and get me to sleep with him before I left. I had to say no numerous times and threaten to stop talking to him before he finally gave up. We were in separate places at the time, and that gave me added comfort, but it still really angered me that he kept pushing the issue despite how many times I said no. This was sexual aggression, and the fact that I kept saying no, only to be pushed more, was abusive. Whether or not he intended it to be, it was because it disrespected and even disregarded my boundaries. No one has the right to violate someone else's sexual comfort and safety in any way. The act of this in any form is abuse. Plain and simple.

Financial abuse may sound like a strange concept, but sadly it's all too common. This form of abuse begins to make sense in the context of a relationship with an addict when you consider the secret and habit that the addict will go to any lengths trying to protect. If the addict can maintain control of the relationship's finances, his or her access to their chosen substance becomes as easy as breathing. Financial abuse includes not allowing the other person to keep their own money, controlling bank accounts, and restricting access, confiscating the person's paychecks and any other forms of income, and in the most severe cases can even spiral into a prostitution situation.

By controlling the finances, the addict essentially also controls what the other person can and can't do. The victim is at the addict's mercy, whether to pay bills, buy groceries, or even provide for children or other family members. It's easy to see how devastating and dominating this form of abuse is on the victim. Further, think about it in the context of the victim trying to leave. What are they able to do without money? It becomes a dangerous situation for the victim trying to hide money away with the plan of saving up enough to leave. If found, it escalates the risk of rage-driven violence against the victim. The addict will not give up control of that cash flow without a fight because to do so would also mean a sharply elevated risk of loss of the ability to continue obtaining that substance that they need constant access to. Standing up and speaking up for themselves is hard enough for codependents as it is. In this situation, it's downright terrifying.

Financial abuse is a terrible and restrictive form of control that is very difficult to break free from. Just as there is no single form of abuse, there is no single or decisive way to get away from it. Every relationship, every situation is different and, as such, calls for responses that are specific to them. What works for one may not be feasible or even a safe solution for another. Abuse in any relationship is destructive and devastating, and never okay. While the addict is being driven by the substance-fueled convolution of chemical messages in the brain, this is absolutely not a viable justification, reason, or explanation for abuse. This chapter was considerably shorter than the previous ones, and I anticipated that that would be the case. While the specifics of abuse and detailing the picture of what it can look like are somewhat black-and-white, I still felt it important to lay it out so that if there are forms of it that I've explained here that you were not aware existed but that you recognize in your relationship with your addicted loved one you now have the understanding of what you're dealing with so that you can figure out the best and safest way to approach it.

I will say it one more time before closing this chapter because it bears constant repeating --- abuse is NEVER okay. Situations don't matter. So-called reasons don't matter. *It doesn't matter!* **Abuse is never okay!** No one has the right to harm another person, and everyone has the right to live a happy, healthy, and safe life filled with equally healthy and safe relationships.

You don't have to and shouldn't settle for less.

Ever.

Part 1: Final thoughts

Loving an addict is a roller coaster of uncertainty, tension, anxiety, and worry. When you're codependent, those already intense emotions and experiences are compounded. Both the addict and the codependent struggle with severe unhealed inner wounds and are depending on each other for very much the wrong reasons. In no way am I trying to suggest or insinuate that the addict is dangerous or evil, nor am I trying to call out the codependent as weak or submissive. There are exceptions to every rule, naturally, but as a general rule, neither is true in this case. The addict is desperate to fill their wound, and they do so with a substance or behavior that allows them to disassociate from that wound, even if just for a little while.

Unfortunately, more often than not, this substance or behavior also alters their personality and causes them to go to great lengths to ensure that they can remain separated from that pain at any cost, that cost often being hurting others. The codependent is also trying to fill a wound, the wound of not being "enough.". The irony here is that both the addict and the codependent struggle with the same feelings but in different forms and various methods. The codependent, feeling not enough in themselves as people seek out others they perceive to be in need in order to "take care" of them in ways they were neglected of, simultaneously feeding the hope and belief that doing so will bring them the validation and affection that they so desperately crave in the form of appreciation and love from that person to whom they're devoting themselves. Unfortunately, it never works this way when it involves an addict. The addict, in turn, sees the codependent as someone who will go to great lengths to make them happy and take care of them, and while they may not be overtly trying to manipulate, the intention is ultimately there because it's about what they need to do to ensure that they can continue to fill their own need. When the two come together, it's a powder-keg. The codependent twists him or herself inside out, trying to "take care of" the addict because that is the nature of a codependent -— the caretaker, usually to their own detriment. The addict uses whatever means they feel they need to use to ensure that their secret's fragility is not exposed. If the codependent can be made to look crazy, then all the questions and doubt will fall on them instead of the addict.

Unlike narcissists who flat out don't care about anyone but themselves, the addict more than likely *does* care, but they're so entrenched in their addiction that they're unable to see beyond it. No matter how many red flags they see, the codependent is determined to "love the addict healthy." It's not possible, but the codependent can't see that. All they see is someone in need whom they can rescue.

Love should never hurt. Someone who loves you will not abuse you, no matter what the excuse. I don't believe that he deliberately set out to hurt me, but I do believe that he had a tremendous amount of anger and resentment within himself, and the vodka drove it out at the first person on his path — that person was usually me. I'm not making excuses for him. The way he treated me was not okay, and it's going to take me a long time to heal, but the most significant step was getting away. I'm going to get into leaving an addict in the next section. My point, though, is that being an addict did not make him evil. He wasn't evil; he was insecure. Deeply insecure. He came from a childhood of severe and traumatic abuse, and while I won't go into detail about it because it's not my place, I will say that what he experienced was brutal. It was so severe that he was unable to face it and heal. That's why he turned to the vodka. It made those monsters go away, at least for a little while. The problem was that it brought an entirely different monster out — the beast of his anger. Neither of us had any business being in a relationship, but we were drawn to each other as two insecure people with unmet needs. I will be the first to take accountability here and say that the person I became when he drank was not someone I liked. Eventually, I went from rolling over and taking it to yelling back, fighting back, and taking low blows back. This is not who I am, and I hated that it was who I became, but I reached the point where I was willing to do anything to get even a few minutes of silence and relief.

Addiction is painful. Codependency is painful. Bringing the two together is detrimental to both involved, but both can also be healed if wanted enough.

Leaving

9

June 2020

"I'm moving back home.".

I could see the sadness fill his eyes even as the tears rose in my throat and blurred my vision. There was an uncomfortable moment of silence that felt like it lasted forever before he responded, his voice quiet, almost resolved.

"When? When is the last time I'll ever see you again?"

My first instinct was to take the question as an attempt at guilt as that is what I had known from him for the last four years, but if I was going to be honest with myself, I truly didn't know whether or not that was the case this time. I took a deep breath that was unexpectedly painful and tried to choke back the tears enough to be able to speak, but he did again before I could.

"I don't want to lose you."

His voice was soft and sounded small and far away. Something inside me exploded. I could feel the fury filling me and heating my face, and I clenched my fists at my sides to the point where my skin dented.

*"**NOW?!**"* I wanted to scream at him. *"I tried for four years to keep our relationship alive and begged you to get help, and **NOW** you don't want to lose me?!".*

This was the point at which my tears became no longer controllable, and I had to look away from him as they poured down my face so that he wouldn't see them, not that they had affected him to the point of making any difference anyway. I had been begging him throughout our entire relationship to try and get his drinking under control. I had cheered him on when he started on medication that was supposed to block the urge to drink, watched the man I had met five years earlier begin to come back, only to then sink right back down when he decided he didn't like the side-effects, stopped taking it, and slipped right back into his old habits again. I had been telling him for longer than I could remember that I'd stand by him through anything if he would only meet me halfway, but it never happened.

Now, here I was at my breaking point, and it was the first time I had actually seen any emotion on his face. It made me angry. I could feel him looking at me. It felt like a hole being burnt through me. I still hadn't answered his question. I didn't want to. I was exhausted. I was drained. I didn't recognize myself anymore. The acidic burn in my stomach had crawled its way up my throat, leaving a metallically bitter taste in my mouth and making it feel uncomfortably dry and sticky. It couldn't have come to this. How could he have let it come to this?! Our future together was gone, all for the sake of his precious vodka. I realized that the bitterness was as much in my heart as it was in my mouth.

"When?"

His voice broke through again, even as quiet as it was, and I finally forced myself to look at him. As much as I wanted to scream at him, I realized I had also never wanted to put my arms around him more. Wringing my fingers together as if somehow it would ease the tension in the room, I swallowed hard again, barely able to see him clearly through my tears.

"August."

I waited for a response. I waited for an argument. I geared myself up for the guilt.

He merely looked away, and in that moment, I knew he had given up.

I could only pray it wasn't on himself.

Loving an addict is hard. Leaving an addict is excruciating. Whether it's a romantic relationship, family members, or friends, we love them. We want to be there to help them, but we are forced to face the crushing realization that there's nothing more we can do, and if we keep trying, we're going to fall apart ourselves. I reached this point with him as I watched his body begin to deteriorate, giving up the fight against the onslaught of alcohol it had been under siege by for the last four years. I still loved this man. Seeing what his body and mind were becoming due to all of the poison that had built up in his blood and hammered at his organs over the years became more than I could bear.

It was the most painful decision I've ever had to make because it was not what I wanted, but I finally accepted the hard reality that what I wanted and had wanted for us just wasn't going to happen. There's no pain like the pain of watching someone you love destroy themselves and knowing you can't do a damned thing about it. This is the cold reality of addiction, though. *We can't help them.* Codependency makes this truth even more painful, as at our core, who we've defined ourselves to be is created and subsequently shattered by our ability to take care of others. Now, here we are unable to help someone we care about when they so clearly need it. It's a gut-wrenching finality to have to accept. I'll never forget the look on his face when I told him I was leaving. I think it was the first time I saw true emotion from him in almost longer than I could remember. This was the end I had been talking about for a long time now, but I don't think he ever thought I would really follow through. It was not the choice I wanted to have to make. My heart was absolutely *screaming* at me – *"How can you do this?! How can you abandon him? You know how this feels! How can you do it to someone you love?!"*.

I knew it was my codependency trying to push me to give in but having that awareness didn't stop it from hurting. He was dying right in front of me and not doing anything to help himself, and I was dying inside watching it. I don't know if he truly believed he was "fine," as he kept insisting he was, or whether he had just buried himself deeply enough into denial to find a comfort zone, but despite his adamance, his presentation both physically and cognitively told a very different story. I was taken back to the first alcoholic I had been with, and I couldn't for the life of me figure out why I had so much easier of a time leaving him than I'd had trying to leave now. It didn't matter, though. I knew that I only had one option now, and I prayed that maybe there was some hope that if I left and were no longer around for him to fall back on, maybe he would finally begin taking care of himself.

As the day got closer, he continued to deteriorate. The seizures became more frequent. His ability to speak clearly, contribute to conversations, and often even make any sense at all declined. He had noticeable trouble walking or even standing without having to grab on to something to steady himself. I wanted to believe that this was just another attempt at guilt to try and get me to stay, but you can't fake physical debilitation, and he was clearly becoming increasingly debilitated as time went on. *Maybe I should stay,* I began thinking to myself. *Maybe now that he's in this condition, he'll start to realize how much help he needs.*

I was fooling myself.

The days grew into weeks, and as they did, I found myself constantly asking him what he was talking about because he wasn't making sense or even using actual words at times and trying to talk him down from anger that I couldn't even pinpoint the reason for because he had taken something completely benign as a personal attack and was defending himself in a non-existent argument. I had never seen him like this before, and I realized that for the first time in four years, I honestly couldn't tell whether he was drunk (he had never been this bad when drunk before, and he had certainly never shown any potential cognitive concerns!), or whether his functionalities really were beginning to crumble from years of alcohol toxicity. It scared me. It hurt my heart. *How could this not scare him into realizing he needs help?!*

Yet it didn't, or if it did, he never let on to me. He stood firmly in his "Sweetie, I'm fine" defense, and I truly couldn't tell whether he was that out of touch with the condition he was so clearly in or whether he was still just hell-bent on lying to me because even after four years he continued to refuse to accept that I could tell when he was sober and when he wasn't. I've said it before, and I'll keep saying it, *we can't love them "better,"* and the harder we try, the more we hurt ourselves. Caring about an addict is difficult enough as it is, as we are literally helpless to do anything for them. As codependents, though, we are so driven by that deep intrinsic need to help, "rescue," and take care of others that when we're not able to, it leaves us feeling like we've failed on the most crucial and irreversible level. We internalize the responsibility for the well-being of others and are emotionally demolished when we can't meet that burden, even though it was never ours to carry to begin with.

I had poured my entire heart into doing everything I thought I could for him, yet here we were staring down the end of everything, and though I knew there was nothing more I could have done, it didn't stop me from feeling like there had to have been if I just tried a little harder — fought a little bit harder. That codependent wound inside me was exposed and bleeding, and for the longest time, I believed that the only option I had for stopping the gush was to bandage the wound by trying even harder to take care of him. I was at the point now, though, where I realized that I did have another option because my own bandage had fallen off. I just wasn't sure I was strong enough to follow it through. The thought of it made me feel selfish and even narcissistic. Was that thinking logical? Of course not, but at this point, logic had a minimal voice over the intensity of my emotions. The thought of leaving him, especially knowing, and seeing how sick he was, consumed me with guilt, fear, and worry. What would happen to him if I weren't here to help him (There went that codependent voice again, assuming the ability to and responsibility of making sure that he was okay, even though he was a grown man who for all intents and purposes should have been able to take care of himself!)? Would he end up homeless? Would he potentially end up in prison or dead? How could I let any of this become a risk?

The answer to that is both simple and complicated:

Because it wasn't up to me to control what happened to him.

That may seem like a harsh interpretation of codependency, but that's exactly what we try to do if you think about it. By trying to ensure the well-being, safety, health, etc. of others, we are essentially exerting control over their situation to know they're okay. As altruistic and genuine as the intentions are, that doesn't make them healthy, and in this case, they're not, for them or us. Think about it. What are we truly doing to help them by protecting them from their choices? In my mind, I was keeping him safe, but at what point did that responsibility become mine to assume? I believed that because I loved and cared about him so much, I should do whatever I could to make sure he was okay. There is nothing wrong with that desire in and of itself but protecting someone from their own consequences enables them to continue engaging in those behaviors that cause them and everyone else around them harm.

So, what option was I left with now? I had only one -- the one that I didn't want to think about; that neither of us wanted to think about. It was the one I had decided on now, though, and I knew that the worst thing I could do for either of us was to turn back. *I had to leave.* It was everything I didn't want to think about, but he had decided to remain active in his addiction, which left me no choice in my own decision. The reality of it was so sharply and overwhelmingly painful that even just the thought of what I was about to do brought me to tears that I was unable to hold back. Despite that I knew I was finally getting away from the yelling and screaming, the name-calling, the false accusations, and all of the stress and hurt that had come with our relationship over the last four years that unhealed Codependent inside me chastised and berated me for doing to him what had caused the wound in me, to begin with. *I was abandoning him.* I was turning my back on someone I loved. What kind of person was I?!

This is why it's so excruciatingly painful for a codependent to leave a relationship. We're not heartless monsters, but we feel like we are. It's difficult for us to put ourselves first as it is because we have this deeply rooted internal belief that we just as ourselves are not "enough," but to put ourselves first in a situation in which someone we care about is suffering?! Absolutely unforgivable in our minds and hearts! It's not wrong, but it feels wrong. Very, very wrong. The concept of self-preservation that is so intrinsic to most people leaves a sick, stale taste in our mouths. That was the point I was at when I forced myself to make the decision to leave. The months leading up to it seemed to move in slow-motion, and I had moments when I wasn't sure if I wanted them to speed up or slow down. Did I want to finally get away and out of there, or did I want just a little more time to try and "help" him? Did I want my freedom so I could heal, or did I want to keep fighting for an "us" that, on a logical level, I knew could never exist as long as he remained active in his addiction? His promises had stopped holding any meaning such a long time before that, as one after the other disintegrated into nothingness without any change.

Looking at myself in the mirror, I didn't recognize the face staring back at me. There was darkness under my eyes from seemingly endless nights without sleep and emptiness *in* my eyes from years of waging war on a demon I'd never have been able to defeat because it wasn't mine to fight to begin with. My skin, which had always been bright and healthy due to my obsessive care and determination to keep it so, was now pale and dull, and suffering from dryness that had never been an issue before. My hair was falling out in clumps, and even just brushing my fingers through it seemed to break it. My lips were cracked from being bitten continuously. I had lost weight, and while usually, this would have been a good thing being too nauseous from anxiety to eat most of the time was not the way I wanted to do it. Most of all, though, I could see hopelessness and the grief of knowing that nothing was going to change. I had fought so hard for him — for us, and now it felt like it had all been for nothing.

Addiction is brutal in its grip on the addict and brutal in its wake on those who loved the addict and are forced to detach. It's referred to as "detaching with love," but it doesn't feel like that's what we're doing at all. *How can we call it love if we're walking away?* I know this is a question that echoed so loudly in my head for so long that I caught myself starting to ask it out loud just to get the noise in my mind to stop. I'm going to play devil's advocate with this question because that's what I had to hear myself before I could finally begin to look at the situation differently:

How can we call it love if we're standing in the way of them taking care of themselves?

I can almost *hear* the screams of readers wanting to throw me and this book into a pit of fire for what I just said, but if we're going to be completely honest with ourselves even though we have the best intentions at heart when we twist ourselves inside out for our addicted loved ones how are we helping them learn to take care of themselves and get healthy if we keep shoving the pillow under them every time they get close to rock bottom? Rock bottom is a scary concept when we think of someone we care about being there, but addiction doesn't give up without a fight, and for an addict to reach the place of being ready to fight, they typically first have to lose everything. Their lives have to become so uncomfortable that they will do anything they have to do to change it. Under the overly protective wing of the codependent, they don't have to worry about ever reaching this place because they know their loved one will be right there to cushion any potential blows.

It's such an unhealthy and uncomfortable catch-22 for the codependent because there will be discomfort involved either way. If they let go and walk away, they have to face the pain of that wound being torn open and the feelings of having abandoned their loved one that come with it, usually sending them careening right back to their own unresolved trauma. If they stay, they continue to face the struggle of caring about and taking care of the addict who, unless something severe happens, is not likely to show any interest in changing or going into recovery. When I decided I needed to leave him, he was not only clearly unhealthy, but he was also unemployed, broke, and homeless, going from hotel to hotel when he had the money to do so. This pushed my codependent tendencies to the breaking point, and I realized that the only way I was going to get out of and away from that relentless internal need to "protect" him by paying for rooms for him was to get far enough away that I would literally and physically be unable to help him. From 1,800 miles away, I wouldn't be able to show up at a hotel and give them my card for incidentals, and there would no longer be the option for him to show up on my doorstep. Everything in me was shrieking at me that I needed to stay because if I weren't there to help him, he would wind up on the street or dead -- more of that contorted codependent thinking at work!

Nevertheless, he depended on me —- and there was the entire problem. He *depended* on me. Over the years, I had shown him that I would always be there to rush right in and catch him before he fell, and I knew now that not only had that not helped him, but quite the opposite. I was standing in his way. He had become so comfortable in the confidence that I was right there that he didn't take any responsibility for his life and the shape it was in on himself. Living in hotels was comfortable? Well, maybe not, but it was certainly likely to be a hell of a lot more comfortable than sleeping on the street, and if he had the roof over his head and still had money in his own pocket, guess where that money could (and did!) then go?! This war inside me – and it *was* a war; a relentless, unforgiving war of logic versus emotion, head versus heart, what I knew to be true versus what I wanted to be true was wearing me down, even after I thought I had decided to leave. I still had two months in front of me to waffle back and forth. Was I selfish? *Was* I abandoning someone I cared about when they needed help more than ever? Of course not, but it felt like I was — even though it's impossible to abandon someone who has already for all intents and purposes abandoned themselves, and he had. It was obvious in everything he was doing, everything he wasn't doing, and for everything *I* had tried so desperately to do for him, it was ultimately for nothing because *he* wasn't ready to get help and get better.

Now here I was, staring down a result I never wanted. The truth is that I was so overcome by the pain and guilt of this decision that even the *thought* of telling him goodbye buckled me into a well of tears all over again. I knew, though, that if I went back now, that was it. I'd be stuck. This was my one chance to get out so that I could begin to heal, and I had to do that.

I was lucky that I didn't need to worry about violence leading up to or after leaving. There were far too many factors working against that happening, not the least of which was the fact that I'd be almost 2,000 miles away in another time zone and surrounded by family and friends who were already feeling very protective. Unfortunately, though, the reality is that often *the* most dangerous time for a person leaving a relationship in which there has been abuse is after they leave because the other person has now lost control and lashes out from that bruised ego. I wasn't afraid of my ex physically, even though he had put his hands on me twice in our four years together. Still, I also knew that my entire saving grace would be in getting not just away but *far* away. He didn't have a license or a vehicle, so I knew once that distance was there, that was it. It would be done. Completely. I don't want my situation to cause complacence, though. I feel it's necessary to be transparently honest when dealing with this because there *are* risks involved, and as I discussed earlier, alcohol and substances tend to drastically alter both personality and behavior, and typically not for the better.

Safety planning is not just some plot twist created for movies and television. It is real, and in relationships in which abuse has occurred, it is also critical. Victims must seek out help and support because the danger level escalates once they leave. One study reviewed by the Women's Journal of Health showed that as low as 11.5% of women leaving an abusive relationship did *not* experience any violence or harassment after separating from the abuser for up to three years (McFarlane, Nava, Gilroy, & Maddoux, 2015). Think about that number. *11.5%!* At the risk of insulting your intelligence, dear reader, that means that nearly **90%** of women experienced some form of retaliative violence from their abuser after they left. That paints a startlingly and equally frighteningly clear picture of the reality of domestic violence after the victim has left. With this in mind, it may seem hopeless, but I promise you it isn't. I can tell you that I was able to get away from my first abusive partner when I was only 22 and with the help of a domestic violence counselor and a safety plan. Again, wanting to remain completely honest, that ex did stalk me for nearly a year after I left, but I remained physically safe from him once I left the relationship.

So, what might a safety plan look like?

It's not so much what it looks like that's important, because really it can look like any comprised list. What's most important in a safety plan is *the plan.* That may sound a bit redundant, so let me elaborate.

A safety plan is a personalized plan a victim will create, typically with a domestic violence counselor that will help them increase safety while in an abusive relationship and continue to remain safe both while getting out of the relationship and once they are out of it. Since each relationship is different, each safety plan is different, tailored to the relationship's circumstances and situations. What's workable for one relationship or plan may not be feasible or even safe for another. Admittedly, I remember very little of the safety plan I created with my domestic violence counselor at the time because it was 20 years ago, but I do remember that it involved having codewords with certain people in my life, which they would understand as meaning that I needed help when I spoke them, and always keeping three to four quarters either in my pocket or in the side panel on the driver's side door of my car in case I needed to use a payphone to call for help. I also remember how petrified and overwhelmed I felt, being that this was the first abusive relationship I had ever experienced, and I was barely 22 years old (he was 10 years older than I was). It's important to determine what will be viable and helpful for your specific situation, always keeping your safety the priority. Domestic violence counselors are trained in helping clients build safety plans that will help them protect themselves throughout and immediately following an abusive relationship.

Safety plans are an utterly invaluable protective tool to help you maneuver the treacherous path of an abusive relationship from start to finish. I speak from personal experience when I tell you that having one in place really offers an extra security level. Just be sure that if you keep a copy with you, you keep it somewhere where your abuser won't/can't find it.

Once again, I want to be sure I emphasize that I am in no way suggesting that *every* relationship with an addict is abusive or will become so. A relationship in which addiction is involved is absolutely at a more heightened risk for violence just by the nature of the changes that occur in the addict, but even with that being said, it still does make abuse an automatic experience. The bottom line is that addiction is just not black and white, and neither is abuse. It would be far easier to proactively address and possibly eliminate if it were. The more you know about it, though, the better able you will be to both recognize the signs of it in your own relationships and reach out for the support and resources you need to get safe, heal, and take your power and your life back after an abusive experience.

August 2020.

"It's okay, kid."

I had felt the tears begin to burn in my nostrils as we pulled out onto the highway to begin the arduous two-and-a-half day drive back home, but I was easily able to distract myself by comforting my cat, who was tucked into her kitty condo in the backseat and fiddling mindlessly with the air conditioner to hold the 100° day at bay. I didn't really feel anything as we pulled out of the parking space of the apartment I shared with my ex for the last two years, and my emotions held off as we passed by the street where the 7-Eleven was that he had worked at a few times. I even cringed as we drove by the liquor store that knew him by name because he went in there so much. I was good. I was fine. Sipping on a bottle of water, nibbling on some peanuts, talking to my dad, and watching the city I had lived in for the last three years pass by for the last time, I was fine.

"Welcome to Nebraska"

It was the last thing I saw before my eyes filled with so many tears that I couldn't see or take a deep enough breath to pull them back. Suddenly it was real. Painfully and undeniably real. I had just left it behind; left *him* behind. The grief shook my insides, leaving me stricken and reeling, and I had to remind myself that I was driving and still had to watch the road. I felt my father's hand on my shoulder and fought desperately to lean into the comfort he was trying to give me, but the pain was relentless and piercing. Before I knew it, I was crying with such intense force that I found myself praying that it would just stop my heart. The reality that I had just physically left the state drove home that it was really over, and that gut-wrenching feeling that I had just abandoned someone I cared about so much swept through me like a tidal wave. I could feel the pain in my chest as if my heart were literally splintering down the middle. I felt my father patting my arm, and I could hear him telling me it was okay and that it was okay to cry, but even though he was sitting right next to me, he sounded miles away. Something inside me screamed at me to turn around, telling me that I could still change it and be there to help him, but that was no longer an option, and I knew it. That should have made it easier. Knowing that it was behind me should have made it better, but it seemed only to serve that wretched gnawing guilt that was already tearing a path of nausea through my stomach on its way to a heart that was already weak and tired and ready to stop beating completely.

"Do you want me to drive for a while?"

I shook my head, and even that felt like an effort. As challenging as driving was, I knew that just sitting there with nothing to focus on would make the pain a hundred times worse because all there would be to do was think. God knows in the four years with him, I had experienced what I was sure was every kind and depth of pain — but I was wrong. The last time I felt this kind of encompassing pain was when I found out my friend Justin (The unfortunate friend who was the first to get the brunt of my yet unrecognized at the time codependency?) had a girlfriend, and that was more than 20 years ago. Now, here I was again, a lifetime later thrown back to that devastated 20-year-old, only *I* was the one doing the abandoning.

"You're *going to be okay, kid.*"

Even at 42, I still found comfort in my father calling me "kid." I tried to push out a smile and hoped it was enough of one that he actually saw it. I knew he knew I was hurting, but for some reason, I still tried not to show it. Not surprising, given the hell I had just come out of, but even so, this was my *father*. He represented all that was safe and protective in my life since I was a child. It didn't matter. The damage was done, and now I had to relearn how to feel safe expressing my feelings. Looking in the rear-view mirror, I sucked in another painful breath as my former state grew smaller and smaller behind me until it was finally gone completely.

Gone completely. Just like everything I had spent four years fighting for. I was safe now, but at what price and whose expense?

Is the codependent thinking in that memory obvious? There I was, finally escaping what had been years of pain and abuse, and yet my first concern was how *my* choice could potentially adversely affect **him**. This is at its core what makes leaving an addict (or anyone "in need") so devastatingly painful for a codependent. We know the crushing feeling of being abandoned, and yet now we're (at least in our own minds) doing it to someone else. It often takes loved ones multiple times to finally break the trauma bond and separate from the addict because we're so enmeshed with them and razor-focused on their needs that we've allowed ourselves to believe that we're their last hope. Sheesh! Talk about a hefty burden!

The thing of it is, though, we **can't** be their last hope. **They** have to be. **They** have to be ready, **they** have to want it, and **they** have to do it. There is no part of that progression that we can take responsibility for (Control of. We may hate it but come on now. I've already talked about how codependency is a means of maintaining control (to ultimately protect ourselves). Before you get defensive and indignant, yes, there are, of course, counselors, therapists, and others trained to provide services to addicts. Yes, there are support groups designed to promote abstinence and clean, healthy living, but what do they all have in common? *The addict. The addict* has to take the first step and reach out for counseling. *The addict* has to be receptive to and active in their treatment. *The addict* has to seek out support groups or other means of further positive redirection. *The addict, the addict,* **the addict.** It all comes down to them and how not just ready but willing they are to do whatever it takes to get and stay sober.

We're not off the hook either, though, my fellow codependents! If we're going to be honest with ourselves, we need help, too –- and that's not a bad thing! The need for mental health treatment is often seen as some kind of subhuman weakness or flaw. That's as ridiculous as it is illogical. We *are* flawed. We all have issues, wounds, and demons. As codependents, how much good can it really do to get away from a toxic relationship if we don't then seriously evaluate ourselves and try to figure out the source of the wound or wounds that keep pulling us back into these patterns so that we can correct them and ultimately have healthy relationships? We may as well just park ourselves in a canoe on a lake with only one oar. It's the same concept: circles, circles, and more circles. We never actually *get* anywhere. I'm not a religious person, but there is a lot of truth to the serenity prayer that is such a steadfast cornerstone of the Alcoholics Anonymous 12-step program – "Grant me the serenity to accept the things I cannot change, *the courage to change the things I can,* and the wisdom to know the difference." Think about it. Leaving a toxic relationship with an addict is a healthy step, yes, but what good is it going to do if we don't then follow it by addressing the wounds in ourselves that keep creating that toxic pull, to begin with?

The fact remains, though, that leaving is hard. Of course, it is. We care about them. We want what's best for them, and chances are we've twisted ourselves to the point of breakage trying to advocate for them even though most of the time they're not advocating or even fighting for themselves. If there are children involved, it makes the picture even more complicated. As codependents, their lack of willingness to get better somehow becomes *our* failure — but it's not. That's like saying we're the reason our partner got a cavity. *They* didn't keep up with their oral care, but it's *our* fault that their tooth rotted as a result.

Huh?! There isn't a shred of logic in that series of events, nor is there a shred of logic in taking responsibility for someone else's unwillingness to stop making unhealthy choices. I'm by no means saying or even suggesting that this somehow makes leaving easier. It absolutely does not. Still, there often comes the point at which we realize that their ship is sinking, and if we don't grab a lifejacket, we're going to drown right along with them — and knowing us, probably while trying to keep *their* heads above water. Wanting to help someone is admirable, but when we start trying to force "help" on other people the way we think it should be done regardless of whether or not they are willing to accept it, it goes from helping to controlling, and that's neither admirable nor our right no matter how much we try to tell ourselves that what we're doing is "out of love." That may be, but just as we don't want to be controlled by the choices and behaviors that come with their addiction, they don't want to be controlled by the demon of our need to "help" them in the ways we think they should be helped. On either side, the picture sucks, but what it comes down to is that the *only* person we can or have the right to control is ourselves.

The bottom line is that for a codependent, leaving any relationship, let alone one in which we feel that the other person *needs* us, is an emotional Molotov cocktail of guilt, fear, grief, and pain. Gee, it sounds like a real picnic in the park, doesn't it? Is it any wonder we have such tremendous difficulty walking away? It took me nearly a year when I seriously first started thinking that I needed to leave him to finally do it. I went through jobs because the fighting at home was so bad that it kept me awake at night, oftentimes all night, leaving me unable to function the next day. Finances were a constant struggle for obvious reasons. I was depressed. Exhausted, drained, and depressed. I loved this man very much, and I knew he was capable of being sober — he was sober when we met. That seemed like a lifetime ago, though. When my breaking point hit, it hit hard. He had started having alcohol withdrawal seizures at least once a month. They were terrifying to witness. He would make this horrible sound; I don't even know how to describe it, really. I want to liken it to the feeling of being shot in the chest for some reason.

The first time it happened, in 2019, I didn't know what the hell was happening. By the time I reached the bathroom, he was on the floor, seizing, with blood coming out of his head from where it smashed it on the toilet paper holder when he fell. I was absolutely petrified. I called 911, and then my boss in a panic, telling her I'd be late coming in and what had just happened, and then waited there feeling utterly helpless until the EMTs showed up. Once they got him conscious, he couldn't even tell them what year it was or who I was. He was weak and spacey.

Sixteen months later, here we were again. The first time, he hit the ground outside on the deck while smoking a cigarette, after spending all day vomiting violently. It was a year later in June. My mother's birthday. That's how I remember the date so vividly even now. By the time I got outside, his eyes were back in his head, and he was stiff and shaking. The second time, on the 4th of July, he didn't even make that horrible sound. I happened to look over, and he was already falling off the bed. I couldn't get over to him fast enough to keep him from hitting his head on the radiator. Both times, I pleaded with him to get help. Both times the diagnosis was alcohol withdrawal. My breaking point had come by this point, and I had told him I was moving back home - alone. He had three more seizures between the day I left and the day I cut off all communication. *Three.* Each time I implored him to go to the doctor and get his bloodwork done because the signs of the impact the alcohol was having on his liver were brutally physically apparent. Every time, I got that same response that made me twitch from hearing it so many times before. By the second seizure, he had bruises all over his legs that he couldn't explain. He couldn't walk. He could barely put sentences together. His body was dying and screaming at him for mercy, and he was ignoring it, or maybe he was aware but in denial. I honestly don't know. All I *did* know was that I couldn't do it anymore. As much as I wanted to be there for him emotionally, it was just too much if he wasn't going to do anything to help himself.

As I said earlier, this was a heartrending decision, not one I wanted to make, but he left me no other choice. I couldn't sit by and watch him die and not even do anything to try and save himself. There is no pain like the pain of watching someone you care about kill themselves and not even try to find a lifeline. As a codependent, the inner war in me erupted into a barrage of guilt-trips and self-loathing. "*You **know** how it feels to feel abandoned. You **know** how it feels to feel like you're not important to anyone. How can you do this to someone you love?*". It was like I was my own captive, and I was beating myself around the clock for an answer that it wasn't even possible for me to know. The more I watched him deteriorate, the more ruthless that war became. The battle of head versus heart is a true war zone for the codependent. It's not that we lack logic. It's just that our feelings' intensity and that dominating need to rescue and protect - to "love them healthy" ferociously override it. How can we help someone else become healthy when we're not even healthy ourselves, though? Thus, the cycle continues. The substance is their distraction from their pain, and *they* are ours. He was burying his demons with vodka. I was burying my unhealed inner wounds by focusing on him. He pulled away from himself by drinking. I pulled away from myself by "taking care" of him. A man in his 40s, and here I was, trying to protect and take care of him like he was an abandoned puppy. In all truth, I wasn't taking care of him at all, but as long as I was keeping a roof over his head and making sure he was safe (While he, meanwhile, was getting into random fights with people on the street and still drinking! Ahem — paging codependent! Hellooooo!) I felt like I was doing what I should be doing to "help" this man I loved. What was I *really* doing? I was enabling him. Remember that cringe-worthy word from earlier? Oy, what a mess! We were both a mess! It came down to that I couldn't handle the guilt and worry that rose in heavy acidic knots in my stomach every time I thought about what I perceived as abandoning him — i.e., taking care of myself by leaving. Or I *thought* I couldn't handle it. How does the saying go? You don't know unless you try?

Well, here it was. I was staring it in the face. After four seizures over the course of two months, along with his refusal to take care of himself, the option to stay around and watch was not only more than I could handle, but I also realized that it was keeping him from taking the accountability he needed to take to (hopefully!) finally take control of his life. I needed to get the hell out of his way and get him the hell out of mine. That's a rather harsh way to say it, but if we're going for brutal honesty here, that's what it had come to. We were not only not healthy for each other, but we were in each other's way. I was in the way of his possible recovery, and he was in the way of my ability to live a happy and peaceful life. Again, does that realization make the thought of leaving easier? Not even a little bit, but it was one that I had to accept, nevertheless.

I wish I could describe what I saw in the last months before I left. Maybe it's better that I can't because seeing someone you love in that condition is not something I'd wish for anyone to have to endure. I described it, yes, but there was so much more to it. The bruises on his legs were large, dark, and angry and spanned the length of both legs all along the front. He couldn't explain or even remember how he got them. They petrified me, though, so I researched and found that such bruises are one of the earliest signs that the liver is starting to shut down. His skin had become pale and dry and yet still somehow looked uneven, and he seemed to scratch at his arms a lot. His eyes were dull and tired, and I couldn't see him in them anymore. They just looked sad and hopeless, and it broke my heart. This man who was once an endless well of energy now could barely balance without having to hold on to something to make sure he didn't fall, and when he walked, it was one slow step at a time, stopping after each one as if he had to take a breath or remind himself how to take another one. He was already thin, but now it no longer seemed proportionate to his height, and I knew he was barely eating. He complained of chest pain and stomach cramps but refused to do anything about them. He was making less and less sense when he talked, and that was when he could put thoughts into sentences at all and still make sense. Watching him deteriorate gave me the most helpless and hopeless feeling. Even after his accident when he smashed his head on the sidewalk while walking to my place, he still insisted on going right back to the hotel the day he got released from the hospital, instead of staying over at least a night to rest and let his head heal even just a little. I think it was at that point that I really realized that he just was not ready to get better. *Really?*

You might be thinking; It *took you until then to realize it?* Therein is the complication of loving an addict, particularly as a codependent. Did it take me until that point to realize it? No, of course not. Did it take until that point to *accept* it? Yes, and there it is. Realization and acceptance are two very different things. You can realize something without accepting it, but you can't accept something you refuse to realize. Realizing that he was not ready to get sober came a while before this experience, but it was only seeing in front of me what it was doing to him and hearing him say he wasn't going to get help that finally drove me to *accept* that everything I had done and everything I might try to do from that point forward would likely be for nothing. I realized that I needed to focus on myself and my own healing, and I *accepted* that the only way that could truly happen was if I completely removed myself from the situation by moving back home. Healing would not and could not happen where I was because I was still accessible to him, and I knew that for my codependency, that meant that I would continue to try to find ways to "help" him, despite the truth of the situation that I already knew. There it was. I needed to leave, and I mean **leave** as in get far, far away.

Part 2: Final thoughts

I know that this section was considerably shorter than Part 1 and likely will be equally short compared to the coming section, but there isn't a lot of discussion that can be done around the subject of staying or going. It all comes down to the individual situation. Leaving may not be an option for some, and that's okay. I'm going to discuss some options for relationships in which communication is necessary (such as co-parenting) in coming chapters, but it absolutely is possible to emotionally detach from an addict and still be able to communicate about necessary issues without allowing them to gaslight or otherwise manipulate you. I'm not going to lie to you --- it's not easy, but it is doable, and like setting boundaries, it becomes easier the more you do it.

Whatever you decide to do, please be gentle with yourself. What you're dealing with is a difficult and painful situation no matter which way you go, and if you're also struggling with codependency, it can be damned near debilitating. Seek support and guidance from trusted people in your life. Come up with a plan based on your situation. Decide what you need to do in order to find and maintain peace in your life regardless of the addict. There is no be-all/end-all rulebook when it comes to managing relationships with addicts. If you need to leave, please make sure you do so safely. Engage help if you need to. While I could have packed up my cat and my stuff and made the 1,800-mile trek home myself (god knows I've done it before!), it was *FAR* easier having my father there, not just for the moving but more importantly emotionally. I needed that support, and I had it. It made a huge difference. If you have that option, I implore you not to refuse it to yourself. There's no reason to go through such a painful situation alone if you don't have to.

Listen, there's no easy answer here. There's so much intense emotion involved in loving an addict, and when codependency is thrown into the mix, it can be downright torturous. We want to believe we can love them better, and we can't. They want to believe they can continue to use and still have what they want, and they can't. Can relationships be maintained with the presence of an addiction? Yes, but I absolutely will not say that these relationships can "work" because they're already bruised with dysfunction and toxicity on their face. Addicts are not bad people, but they are tangled up with substances that cause them to make bad choices and engage in bad behaviors. Codependents are not weak people, but their past experiences have left them in a place where they only feel strong and whole in themselves if they're focusing their entire existence on caring for someone else also perceived to be in need. These are two conditions that are unfortunately very toxic when they are brought together, but that doesn't mean that either is bad. If leaving this kind of relationship will allow you to heal and find peace again, then, by all means, do so if it's an option, but please be gentle with yourself. You're not a failure, just as the addict is not evil. You can't fail at something that was never your responsibility to begin with. Please remember that so that no matter what you decide to do in your relationship, you can feel confident in your decision, as well as your ability to protect and take care of yourself.

Letting Go

11

A week after getting home.

"How are things going with him?"

I could hear the worry in her voice, and I felt terrible. Lynn was a kind, generous, and genuine soul who cared deeply and unconditionally for the people in her life. Even though initially she had been a supervisor for a past job, she and I became fast friends, and I valued and respected her and her opinions very much, so hearing the concern in her voice was not something I could or wanted to overlook or ignore. She knew everything that had gone on with him, and she knew I was now home but had not cut him off completely. She knew the guilt and worry I struggled with, and as always, she was compassionate and empathetic, but I knew she was also very worried about my emotional state.

"Um. He's still in hotels. He says he's okay. He keeps apologizing and telling me how much he misses me".

I sounded so pathetic to myself, but I knew Lynn wouldn't see it the same way. She had an amazing capacity for understanding and the ability to put herself in someone else's shoes. Her voice was gentle when she spoke again, but I could hear the urgency in it.

"I know this is so hard for you, but please, Meredith., you know he's not going to change. This isn't good for you. You can't heal as long as you're still talking to him. Please."

She hadn't elaborated on what the "please" was pleading with me for, but she didn't have to. I knew. It was something I knew deep down I would inevitably be likely to have to do if I ever wanted to be free of the constant guilt and worry and the continued feelings of responsibility for making sure he had a roof over his head and was safe. It was something I knew I'd inevitably need to do if I ever truly wanted to heal from my codependency. I was trying so hard not to cry, but I knew she knew how emotionally raw I was. I never felt like I had to hide my emotions from her. As the tears surged into the pit of my throat and began to sting in my nose, I caught a choked sob and squeezed my hands together as if that would somehow magically make it stop.

"I just don't want him to end up on the street."

"It's not your problem, dear."

The words were harsh, but only because I knew how true they were, and her voice was as gentle as it always was. There wasn't an ounce of cruelty or insensitivity in her words. There never was. It just wasn't who she was. Suddenly I was assaulted by all these horrible images of him in my head — scraggly, dirty, hungry, sleeping on sidewalks, or park benches. It was enough to knock down what remained of my self-control, and I started crying. There was just no way I could fix this, as I had been wrenching myself inside out trying to do for the last four years. Either I kept communication with him, knowing I'd be listening to a repeating record of him telling me he had slept on the street the night before, or gotten into a fight with someone and was hurt, had no money for food, or even begging me to "Just get him a few more nights" at the local hotel hoping to be able to appeal to the concern he knew I had for him, or I cut him off and faced the consuming grief that I knew would come with doing that, as well as my own internal struggle with staying firm with it and not relenting just to make sure he was okay.

"Please think about it. You've been through so much already".

Her voice broke through my thoughts, and I closed my eyes for a second as if that would somehow calm me down or redirect the conversation. I loved her for how much she cared. It was a comfort.

I also knew she was right.

Leaving and cutting a loved one off can be two very different animals. Though they may sound like the same thing, one does not automatically lead to the other. For a codependent, leaving a loved one is like walking away from them when they have an open wound. *Cutting off* a loved one is the equivalent of seeing them get shot and not being able to get to them in time to save them, only we're also the one who shot them. That may sound dramatic, but it's really how it feels. Staring the reality of what I had to do in the face (so to speak) made me feel like all the oxygen had been sucked out of my lungs, and now I was gasping. I could restore the oxygen by continuing to talk to him, but that ability to breathe would only last until the first time he told me he was sleeping on the street or that he wasn't eating or begged me to pay for a hotel room for him, and then I'd be back to hyperventilating again. This was the cycle I had been in for longer than I could remember; this vicious cycle of control disguised as worry and fear. Remember earlier, when I talked about how the codependent's need for control is the way we (at least in our own minds) ensure that we aren't hurt. After all, if we have control over a situation, we decide what direction it goes in and how, except that's not how it works when talking about *other people's* choices. I had thrown myself into this seemingly endless loop of efforts to ensure that he had shelter, and though it truly did come from a place of genuine care for his safety and well-being, it also gave *me* the reassurance of knowing that he was safe. I needed that reassurance because it meant that I was doing what I should be doing to help someone I cared about. In the back of my mind, I was well aware of enabling and how easy a trap it was to fall into. I also knew that I fell into it a long time ago and had been trying to push and claw my way out ever since, but my drive to rescue still had a strong hand over the mouth of my logic, choking off its ability to really make itself known and heard. *He couldn't take care of himself, so it was my responsibility to take care of him.*

The epitome of codependent thinking, right there. Even now, when I was 1,800 miles away, I still felt that desperate need to do what I perceived as 'protecting' him. He was struggling, and I had the ability to help, so it was my responsibility to do so. With that in mind, how in the hell could I even *think* of cutting him off completely? I was all he had! I was the only one still fighting for him -- even though he wasn't fighting for himself. Even from clear across the country, I could still *save* him!

NOPE!

This is one of the most difficult things about codependency. No matter what we do to try and separate from the problem, ultimately, unless we separate from the *source* of the problem, the cycle will continue. I had taken every word Lynn had said to me to heart. I had heard the pleas of close friends imploring me to cut ties and "let him figure out his own shit," as it was put to me so often, but I know how *I* would feel if it seemed like everyone in my world gave up on me. The thought of doing it to him was more than I could stand. Now, you might be thinking to yourself, *"you're putting yourself in someone else's shoes. That's a good thing".* Under normal circumstances, yes. It absolutely is a good thing. Caring about an addict, particularly as a codependent, is anything but a normal circumstance, though. Unfortunately, in this kind of situation, we're bending ourselves into emotional human pretzels trying to put ourselves in the shoes of a person struggling with a demon that we have no hope of understanding unless we're also an addict ourselves. This is not something that we can put ourselves in their place with and continuing to try and do so will destroy us. The only one we can help is ourselves. I know that this is a tough thing to accept, but we have to. *The **only** one we can help is ourselves.* It doesn't mean we don't still love them. What it does mean, however, is that we realize that if we don't love ourselves more, we're going to lose ourselves trying to help them find sobriety that they're not ready for.

The hardest part of this is often the guilt. I know this will be easier for me to say than it will be to accept but cutting off contact with a loved one struggling with addiction is NOT doing something wrong. Further, it's often the only thing you *can* do to help them help themselves. I know that may not make sense on its face but think about it. Think about everything you've done up to this point to try and "help" them. Where has it gotten them? Where has it gotten *you?* My bet would be exhausted, anxious, overwhelmed, and feeling both helpless and hopeless. How does that old Einstein saying go — "Insanity is doing the same thing over and over and expecting different results." ?

It's so, so true here. For weeks, months, even years, we try and try and try — we beg, we plead, we bargain, we get angry, we threaten, we cry, we often put up with terrible treatment, all in the hopes that if we just do enough, just try enough, things will change. Has it worked? I'm betting that the answer is no; otherwise, you probably wouldn't be reading this book now. So, I ask again — where has it gotten either of you? He had literally begun to deteriorate in front of me, and yet all the begging in the world couldn't push him to get help. He wasn't ready, and I was killing myself, waiting for him to be. I'm not saying that cutting off all contact is the *ONLY* option. If you feel you can manage what you're dealing with and still maintain your own health and well-being, please do. As I mentioned in an earlier chapter, for relationships in which cutting off all contact isn't an option, there is a way to do it that will allow you to keep yourself protected. It's called gray rocking. I will go into it in more detail in a coming chapter. There are also apps that provide a service in which you can message back and forth with a former partner about shared parental issues, but that's it. It really just depends on your personal situation and the dynamics of it. If there are no ties that hold you to obligations in the relationship, it makes cutting off contact easier, but it's still not going to be *easy*.

This is why it's important to consider all of your options as they pertain to *your* relationship. This is not a one-size-fits-all situation. You have to be sure that the choice you make is ultimately going to be what is best for **you** (and of course any children involved, if there are any). It's not easy to try and let go of our natural tendencies as codependents to want to keep rushing in and rescuing, but the best thing you can do for a loved one in active addiction is to let them fall, in whatever form that needs to take. I know I struggled with this idea because I was so firmly rooted in the feeling that I'd be abandoning him. It's also the best thing for us, though, because once separated from the situation, we can begin to focus on healing and becoming stronger so that we are better able to attract and recognize healthy relationships in the future and avoid toxic ones. It may not be the choice we wanted to make, but for both our sake and theirs, it's the choice we might *have* to make.

12

August 26, 2020

"I had a seizure last night."

I heard his voice, but I suddenly couldn't feel my own hand holding my phone. It felt like I had forgotten how to breathe, but my heart was pounding so hard I could feel it as if it were slamming against my chest to try and breakthrough it. Here I was, yet again with tears in my eyes over him. I was 1,800 miles away, but that didn't lessen the same familiar ache that squeezed and clenched in the pit of my churning stomach every time he had a seizure or even told me about having one. He was in a hotel room. Alone.

"Are you okay?"

I could barely choke out the question because my throat felt as if a lit match had been tossed into it. I swore it was in that moment that my heart, which had been hammering my chest only seconds before, had now stopped beating completely as if hinging on his response to determine whether or not to start up again.

"I have a headache and a gash on my head. I hit my head on the radiator when I fell".

There it was. Yet another head injury. This was his third one within a one-month timeframe. He had fallen down a flight of stairs at a hotel while still drunk at the end of July and then had a seizure on a walk to my place a few weeks later, which ended in him smashing his head on the sidewalk and being found unconscious by someone having seen the incident and called 911, and now this. I waited for the tears that always seemed to rush into my eyes anytime I heard that he had been hurt because of his drinking, but they didn't come. I felt that same familiar strong ache, but no tears. Was I finally resigned?

"Did you go to the hospital? Did you get checked out?"

I don't know why I did this to myself. I already knew the answer, but I kept holding out hope that he would realize what he was doing to himself and get help. It was wishful thinking then, and it was wishful thinking now. Still, I held my breath and prayed it wouldn't be the same tired and irritating brush off.

It was.

"Sweetie, I'm fine."

I wanted to scream. I don't know why, really. I knew that was what he was going to say. The man had just sustained his third head injury in under two months, but he was "fine." Well, *I* wasn't, and I suddenly realized it and the totality of it more than I had ever been able to up to this point. Something in me broke. He said he had to take care of something with the hotel and would be right back, and we hung up. I sat staring blankly ahead for what felt like a ridiculously long minute, the tears now filling my eyes not because I was upset about what had just happened to him but because I knew that I couldn't take it anymore. I had hoped that putting distance between us would at least make it easier for me to maintain communication because he'd know there would be nothing I could do for him from where I was, but I was wrong.

Heartbreakingly wrong.

My fingers shook as I opened up the email message.

"I can't do this anymore. I care about you, and I can't watch you destroy yourself and not do anything to help yourself. You're an adult, and you have the right to live how you want to live, but I have the right to have peace, and that can't happen if I'm always worried about you. As long as drinking is going to remain a part of your life, then I can't. If you ever get to the point where you're in treatment and getting true help for yourself, please come find me, and I'll stand by you, but as long as things are going to remain like this, I have no choice but to walk away. I'm sorry. I just can't live like this anymore. I still love you. Please know that. I hope one day, you can find help, health, stability, and happiness."

I knew that to solidify it, I had to send it and then block him because if I didn't, I knew he would try to change my mind and get me to stay around. I had to cut off *all* contact, but it was so much easier said than done. I blocked him on social media, then blocked his email address and the number he had been calling me from.

Then I broke. I broke and cried harder than I think I ever have in my life— hard, painful, body-shaking sobs. I collapsed into my pillow and clenched it to my face because I didn't want someone hearing the agony-filled screaming I was doing and thinking something was going on that needed a check-in from the police or the EMTs. This was *not* what I wanted for us, and certainly not how I would have wanted it to end. I felt cruel, heartless, and selfish, cutting off this person I cared about so much without even giving him the chance to respond to what I had said, but I knew where giving him that opportunity would lead. I also knew he would not just give up. That wasn't who he was. What I had just done may have felt like the hardest thing I'd have to go through, but I was very wrong.

2 days later

"Hey. I just wanted to say hi and tell you I love you. I had to sleep on the street last night. I'll probably have to again tonight. I miss you. Call me here and leave me a message, and I'll call you back. Love you, sweetie. Bye."

I had recognized the number that popped up on my caller ID as the number of the local homeless shelter, and against everything in me, I didn't answer and let it go to voicemail. Listening to the voicemail, I collapsed into tears all over again. He was on the street. It had always been my worst fear with him, and now, here it was.

"HE NEEDS YOU! He's on the street! How can you just turn your back?!"

My inner codependent was screaming at me the way he used to scream at me when he was drunk — with all of the same anger and judgment, and then *I* screamed and hurled my favorite pillow across the room, though I knew damn well it wouldn't make anything feel better. I had just abandoned him *again!* I had the chance to help him, and I left him hanging. He had been on the street because of me, and now he will be back there again, because of me. As the tears came faster and harder, I buried my face in my hands, begging for mercy from any god who might be out there to hear me. There was no way I would be able to keep this up -- to keep not talking to him. I had just spent four years with this man. I lived with him for three. The longest we had ever gone not talking was a few days, and now here I was at that point already, and it felt like everything in me was just dying without him.

This is the pain of going no contact as a Codependent.

Please know that I am in no way suggesting that going no contact is easier for people who aren't codependent. Trying to cut someone off who has likely been a central part of your life for a long period of time is one of the most painful things for anyone to have to do. For the codependent, though, it is that old unhealed wound being shredded open to bleed all over again. We failed once, which is what we believe made us unlovable to begin with, and now we're failing again, which reinforces that awful feeling of being unworthy and not enough. It's the repulping of scarred flesh. Writing that sentence even made me cringe, but it's accurate, nevertheless. From that profound feeling of not being enough that codependents function from, giving someone else, let alone someone we care about, a reason to feel the way we were made to feel is akin to validating that we really are worthless and terrible. This is exactly the kind of thinking that pulled us into the toxic relationship, to begin with. We find our worth in others' well-being and care, and who is more in need than an addict?! It stands to reason then that if we "fail" at that, we must be worthless after all. It's a horrible emotional prison to live in.

Back to this, "no contact" thing, though. It sounds basic enough, right? We just stop talking to them. Okay. Seriously. If it were really that easy, would it need to be named? Particularly in this age of technology, there are varying opinions on what does and does not constitute "no contact." There is also the belief that this technique can be used to "win back" a partner.

No, no, no.

That's called manipulation. Using a tool or technique to get someone else to do something we want them to do is manipulation, plain and simple. If we don't want to be manipulated by them, why would it be okay for us to manipulate them?! The "theory" is that by going no-contact for a certain period of time — a month, six months, whatever it is, it will essentially drive the other person to want to reopen the door and reestablish the relationship. Why would you want to be with someone you had to manipulate into wanting to be with you? If you have to basically con someone into wanting to come back into your life, how much of a relationship was there to come back into, to begin with? That's a game. Children play games. If you feel you have to play games to get someone back, you probably shouldn't be in a relationship to begin with because you have more important issues to focus on. No contact used for what it's meant for is a way for someone to separate from a toxic relationship or influence so that they can heal. As you continue to maintain that distance, the pain is given the time it needs to lessen because you no longer have that constant emotional force coming at you.

In all honesty, the deluge of videos on YouTube from people trying to "teach" others how to "use" no contact to "win back" their partners really angers me because not only are they giving false hope, but they're teaching people how to manipulate to get what they want.

If someone you care about tells you they need distance and don't want you to contact them you wouldn't contact them *because* you care about them and respect what they're telling you they need from you. That doesn't mean you cut them off for a month and then come back asking them if they're ready yet. That's like parents taking their child on a trip, and the child constantly asking, " Are we there yet?". Just as the parents will tell the child when they get to where they're going, so too will the other person tell you if or when they are ready to talk to you again. No contact is called that for a reason and should be respected by the person initiating it for however long they need it, even if it's permanently.

When I went no contact with him, I knew that I would need to stick to it indefinitely if I were going to do it. Going backward wouldn't do either of us any good because it would just throw us both back into that broken and toxic cycle that I had spent so long trying to break. It wasn't because I didn't love him anymore. Of course, I did. Most people can't just turn that off. This was the most painful thing I'd had to do in a long time, if not ever, *because* I still loved him, but that's also the reason I knew I had to do it. I talked about getting out of his way, and I knew that this was the only way to do that. As long as he knew he had me to lean and rely on, he would continue feeling no real need to figure out his own situations and learn how to fix them for himself. He had to sink or swim without having me there throwing him lifejackets before his shoulders even went under.

Going no contact seems to mean different things to different people. I'm not sure why but to each their own. With technology being such a primary form of communication, there has been some question about whether or not staying friends on Facebook or Twitter is considered no contact. By definition alone, no, it can't. No contact means exactly that – *no* contact. No texting. No Facebook messaging. No Facetiming. No Twitter or Snapchat. No trolling the person's page to see what they've been up to or who else they might be with. While constantly scouring the other person's Facebook page to "keep up with them" isn't in and of itself a form of contact, it also keeps the wound open by continuing to feed it what it's starving for. It may feel like you're easing the pain, but are you? If you become a regular silent fixture on your ex-partner's page, and by doing so, you see that he or she has begun seeing someone else, what good has that now done for you? I'd be willing to bet it certainly didn't make you feel better. In fact, I'd even go as far as feeling confident in the assumption that it has intensified the pain you were already in because not only were you already feeling rejected, now you're also likely feeling thrown away completely. Discarded. How could that possibly make *anyone* feel good?!

So, I ask again: What good does it do you to loiter around on their social media feeds like a puppy waiting for a treat? You know that treat is never going to come. Deep down, you know it, even if you're not yet able to accept it. Why torture yourself any more than you're already feeling? I know it's hard. Believe me, I know. I had to force myself to unfriend him and block him, and it was excruciatingly painful, but I knew it had to be done if I was going to have any chance of maintaining no contact past a few days. I'm not going to lie to you — I broke down once it was done -- like crumbled. I honestly didn't know if it was something I could be strong enough to maintain, but I also knew I had to. This toxic merry-go-round had been spinning for long enough, and if one of us didn't jump off, we were both going to wind up falling off and hitting the ground hard once we did. There were many times when I considered unblocking him, even if only to reach out and see if he was okay, but I steeled myself against the urge as best I could by trying to distract myself with other things. Rest. Journaling. Calling my brother or a friend. Even playing with the cat. Anything to pull me out of the place my mind was stuck in, so I didn't do something I knew I'd regret later, even if it relieved the pain in and for the moment. That's not to say I didn't find other ways to torture myself. I found myself Google searching his name just to see if anything came up. Was he okay? Was he in the hospital? In jail? Dead? My mind messed with me something fierce with all the possibilities that "could have been" since I walked away. After he called from the shelter, I blocked the number, but I still knew it and could have easily called there and left him a message. I knew he'd have called me back. That wasn't an option. I couldn't allow it to be.

I have to give credit where it's due — I would not have made it through the first month of no contact without my therapist at the time. Kathryn and I had been working together for two years at that point, and when I decided to go no contact, she was right there to cheer me on and encourage me. She helped me survive him while I was still with him, and she was helping me survive myself now that I had separated from him. It was a hard blow having to stop working with her once I moved out of state, but as gracious and kind as she was, she encouraged me to reach out to her through email if I ever felt stuck and needed support. I leaned on her *a lot* in that first month, and it made all the difference in helping me maintain it.

The first question you might be asking with going no contact is *how? How* do I do this? How do I stick to it? Some of the answers might seem far simpler than you'd probably expect.

- **Therapy**. This may sound cliché, but it really is so helpful. God knows, I don't think I could have made it through that first month without Kathryn. It's an outlet, a safe space. I don't for the life of me understand why people scoff at the benefits of it. It's a private place in which you can let those feelings out, and they need to come out so you can heal from them. If ever there was a safe place to let yourself be vulnerable, it's in therapy. Going to therapy is not a weakness. If anything, it shows how willing you are to do anything you can to heal and become strong again, which takes real guts.

- **Journaling.** Again, I know — cliché, but there is something very therapeutic about writing, especially when that writing is about your feelings. It doesn't get any more private than journaling, which also means you don't need to censor yourself. Whether you buy an actual journal, or start a blog, get it out, get it out, get it out. The more you release it, the less power it holds, and in no case is that truer than with emotions. The more you let it out and get it out, the less it stings. I personally love to write (can you tell, after 104 pages?), and in the first days, after I went no contact, I started a blog which I wrote in daily. When I felt weak, sad, angry == whatever it was, I went right into the blog and got it out. As time went on, I realized I wasn't writing in it as much because those feelings weren't nearly as raw anymore.

- **Rest**. Wait -- What? How did that get in there? Well, think about it – what does the body need when it's exhausted? Rest. What could be more wearing on both the mind and the body than constant intense emotion, especially when that emotion is negative? The mind needs rest as much as the body does. You're grieving. You're trying to heal from severe and ongoing trauma. That's a lot for one system to absorb. If your body is telling you it needs to rest, listen to it. Sleep is precious during the grieving process and can also be difficult to get consistently. I can attest to this personally, as even now, I still wake up at least once a night. Rest is absolutely critical to your ability to heal. Don't deny it to yourself. It's the kindest thing you can do for yourself during this time.

- **Support**. Friends. Family. Coworkers. Hell, I have long (and one-sided) conversations with my cat (who just looks at me like I've sprouted a second head). Surround yourself with and lean on emotionally safe people who love you. Let them help hold you up until you're strong enough to stand on your own again. That's what loved ones are for. For me, it was a few close friends, including one I met through a Facebook support group for loved ones of addicts and became fast friends with, and my twin brother, whom I swear should have been paid by the hour for all the times he listened to me cry. They helped me stay strong when I couldn't do it on myself. You're not an island. Don't make yourself one. Why go through it alone if you don't have to?

- **Distractions**. Passions, hobbies, whatever you call them, use them. If you're feeling the urge to break no contact, distract, and redirect. What are some things you enjoy doing? What brings you joy? For me, it was starting this book and baking! Baking brings me tremendous joy, but I stopped doing it while with him because he made it impossible to enjoy it with his constant need to direct, micromanage, and control. I dove back into it full speed once I went no contact because I knew it would bring me that endorphin rush I needed to feel better and pull myself out of the headspace that could drive me to make a bad decision.

- **Physical activity**. I know, I know... (grumble, mutter) *I'm not in a good place right now. The last thing I want to do is exercise*. That's exactly the point. You're not in a good place. Physical activity in any form releases endorphins — you know, those "feel good" chemicals? Studies show that even 30-minutes of aerobic exercise increases the engagement of positive reward responses, leading to a stronger ability to resolve feelings of depression and anxiety (Brush, Foti, Bocchine, Muniz, Gooden, Spaeth, Miller, & Alderman, 2020). That's pretty motivating, no?

- **Self-care, self-care, self-care!** Don't underestimate the importance of self-care! As I told a woman I'm in a support group with — you just walked through and out of a blazing fire. It's going to take a while for those burns to heal. Be the water, not the accelerant. You need to devote yourself *to* yourself right now. Take a bath. Take a nap. Take a walk. Hell, take ten minutes just to scream and throw pillows. Give yourself that unconditional care and concern that you spent so much time and energy giving your addict for so long. While this is common sense for most, it's a foreign and even an uncomfortable concept for the codependent.

*Put **myself** first?! What does that even mean?! I don't want to be selfish.* Listen –- it was pointed out to me years ago that there is a decided difference between selfishness and self-preservation. Doing what you want without any regard for others is selfishness. Protecting yourself from situations and experiences that could (and likely will!) harm you, and that absolutely includes relationships, is self-preservation. That's why we all have those little voices alerting us to red flags when we meet others. The struggle with codependents is the difficulty in trusting themselves at all, let alone with enough confidence to adhere to those red flags before we can get hurt. I can tell you that there were red flags with him very early in the relationship, but because I was so smitten with him, I wanted only to see and believe the good in him, so I did what a lot of us do –- I overlooked the red flags. Brushed them off. Having listened to them would have been an act of self-preservation. It may not have felt good, but it would have protected me from the pain, instability, and trauma I went through for the four years we were together.

- **Feel.** *Oh, man! That's what I'm trying **not** to do!* I get it. I really do. The emotion is so raw that we're willing to do anything to make it stop, but unfortunately, the only way to get past it is to go through it. It sucks. There's no question about that. There are times it feels like that pain is just going to swallow us whole, and we might even wish it would, but we *need* to sit with it, acknowledge it, and feel it so that it can be released. Our addicts poured a lot of toxicity into us. It's not going to disappear overnight, and the only way for the heart to get rid of it is to feel the pain associated with the trauma. When doing no contact, that means experiencing that sharp, consuming agony as the carnage that was left behind once they're gone. It will pass. I promise it will, but you have to be willing to sit with it.

I'm going to be honest with you, while staying no contact does get easier the longer you stick with it, you *will* still have 'those' moments –- those moments when you think of your loved one, and it hurts. I have been no contact with him for almost five months now, but he's still in my thoughts. Those thoughts aren't as frequent as they were a month and a half ago, but they do still happen, and sometimes when they happen, they do still hurt. I call it the " twinge" –- that sudden and sharp ache that sinks from your chest into the pit of your stomach and can almost bring you to the verge of tears. *This is normal!* Of course, you're going to miss them. Of course, you're going to wonder if they're okay.

At the point I finally went no contact, he was homeless, and I knew that cutting him off would mean that he would likely wind up on the street — and he did. I found out that he has basically been on the street since I left, and I can't tell you how sharply that stabbed my heart and even goaded me to break no contact to try and reach out to him -- but I knew I couldn't. Knowing it didn't stop it from hurting, though. Going no contact doesn't mean you stop caring. It hurts my heart to know that he is struggling so much and doesn't even have a roof over his head right now, but I can't let that play into my codependency because it will if I allow it to. I want to hear his voice. I miss it. That's a normal part of grieving a lost relationship. We miss them. It's painful. The thought of him being on the street, sleeping in the cold, going in and out of day shelters just to get a warm shower, having only food stamps for food until his next unemployment payment clears so he can move into a hotel for a few nights -- it's really painful. We never want someone we love to be suffering, but we also can't take responsibility for making sure they're not, especially when they're not making efforts towards the same end.

Logically I understand that he is where he is because of the choices he made, but we already know that for the codependent, logic is the equivalent of the meek kid pushed around by the playground bully, the bully, in this case, being codependency. As an adult, I recognize that he is facing the consequences of his choices, but it's extremely difficult for me not to rush back in and try to help him as a still healing codependent. That is where it becomes so important to engage those actions that I just explored -- therapy, journaling, rest. These are activities and behaviors that give attention to that place in us that is feeling weak and nurtures it with the things it needs to feel strong again *without* falling back into the old and toxic habits just because they're familiar. Familiarity isn't always healthy. This is also where boundaries come back into the picture. Just as we have to set them with our addict while in the relationship, we also usually wind up having to set them after we've walked away, especially at first. For me, that meant blocking all numbers I knew he could call me from, unfriending and blocking on social media, and not allowing myself to contact his mother, whom I still maintained contact with to ask how he was; not that I needed to. She would text me every so often with something she needed for him that she thought I might have or know, and with those texts came updates about how he was — and it was like having my heart broken all over again. The last text even came with a phone number for the hotel he had been staying at that he had asked her to give me in the hopes that I would call him. She said she thought he was "concerned about his things." I had told him right after I left that I had gotten rid of all of his stuff. I recognized what this was. Even so, I now had a way to reach him right in my hand, and I wanted to use it. I *wanted* to call him. My heart was pounding so hard I could hear it in my ears. Suddenly my emotions started feeling raw again. I knew what calling him would lead to, but I missed his voice. Very, very much. I had two choices: call and fall right back into the old patterns just for the sake of being able to hear his voice, or don't call and maintain the no-contact I'd been holding steady in, but once again have to sit with that raw and unforgiving pain.

Then I deleted the number.

It was a painful thing to do, but I knew that stepping back onto that path would ultimately lead me right back down the same dead-end I had finally managed to get myself off of. I needed to maintain that boundary that I had set, even as painful as it was. I deleted the number before I could allow myself the chance to use it. I'll even go as far as admitting that I shocked myself by doing it. I really thought when I saw that number that was it — the no contact I had been trudging through for the last month and a half was down the toilet, and I'd have to start all over again, or worse — right back onto that malfunctioning merry go round I was going. I also knew that the longer I let myself just sit there frozen and think about it, the higher the likelihood that I'd wind up relenting and calling him. That vicious war between head and heart was back in full force, and I had to do something to diffuse it and do it quickly, so I didn't become the casualty.

Once the number was gone, I cried. It hurt. It really hurt. I even had a moment of regret. I knew I did the right thing, but that didn't mean it felt good -- and it didn't. This is why boundaries are so difficult for codependents. They go against everything we believe our worth and " enoughness" to be wrapped up in. Further, I also didn't ask his mother which hotel he was staying at, because she had given me his room number and I knew that if I knew where he was, I could easily look up the hotel's phone number myself and call him. Six months ago, the decision would have almost definitely gone the opposite way because I wasn't yet strong enough to stand firm in the boundaries I tried to set. I was getting there, but still nowhere near in such a place that I could resist temptation when it was staring me in the face. I couldn't believe I had just done what I did. I let myself feel the sadness and do the crying that needed to come with the decision because it was a painful one. Then I reached out to a friend for support, did some more work on this book, and shared my experience in one of my social media support groups, finding comfort and empowerment in the positive responses and affirmations I got back. I sat with the emotions so I could move through and past them, and I did.

Before I close this chapter, I feel the need to re-emphasize one particularly crucial part of managing and successfully maintaining no contact — self-care. People have different reactions to anxiety and grief. In the interest of continued transparency, I found myself engaging in an anxiety-driven behavior that I'd never in a million years thought I'd ever do — picking. I started picking at my arm, to the point where it bled and left red welts. I've studied mental illnesses and disorders for years. I recognized what this was. When I realized what I was doing, it alarmed me, and I immediately reached out to a doctor and my therapist to try and get ahead of it before it got any worse. Self-care. This was not normal behavior for me, and I recognized it as a grief response. I was using it to pull myself out of that mental place that could ultimately drive me to break no contact. My doctor prescribed me anti-anxiety medication and also a sleep aid because I had gone for the last four years having not slept through the night, waking up at least once a night every single night. I started focusing more on this book and on activities that I knew would bring me happiness. The excoriation was my way of expelling the sadness and anxiety of the grieving process I was going through because there was so much intense trauma left in the wake of the relationship. Self-care is so crucially important to the healing process after leaving a relationship in which addiction was involved. If you're also codependent, it becomes that much more important, even as challenging as it is. A strong positive can come from such a negative experience, but it's going to take hard work, and that work *has* to start with self-care. When you're trying to remain in no contact with your addict, self-care is absolutely and unequivocally necessary. You need your care right now more than anyone else.

13

January 2020

"YOU'RE the one with the problem! YOU'RE the narcissist! You know I'm recording everything".

He was off on another drunken tirade again. I had lost track of what the initial so-called "issue" had been. Once he got started, he tended to bumble around on nonsensical weaving verbal paths that a person would have to be able to think at the speed of light (or be as off-kilter as he was!) to make sense of just trying to find the emotional spaghetti that would stick to the other person's wall. I was long past that point.

"*If you say so.*"

I didn't look at him. I didn't acknowledge him past that. It was well past 11:00 pm by this point, and after two hours of him going off, I was exhausted and still trying desperately to get to sleep.

"*Stop SAYING that! That's all you ever say anymore. I'm trying to talk to you, and you just don't say anything, except "If you say so.*"

"*Uh-huh. Goodnight*".

"*No! NOT goodnight! I'm **trying** to talk! See?! This is the problem! YOU are the problem! THIS is why we fight!*".

"*Okay, sleep well.*"

He muttered something under his breath. I had no idea what. I doubt he did either. I knew he was angry. I turned my head away from him, not that that ever stopped him from continuing to yell and scream.

"***Sleep well?!** THAT'S all you're going to say?!*"

"*If you could do the dishes tomorrow, I'd appreciate it.*"

"*Fine. I tried to talk to you.*"

"Okay. Thanks. Night".

He continued to mutter as he got up off the bed and staggered outside to have a cigarette, and I finally took the breath it had felt like I'd just spent the last two hours holding and tried to get to sleep before he came back inside.

I know I went back a bit in the time frame, but there's a reason. In a few chapters in this book, I have mentioned there are ways to essentially "emotionally check-out" when dealing with intrusive behavior, such as what I just illustrated. One of these ways is a method called "gray-rocking," and it's pretty much what it sounds like — you become a rock. -- an emotional rock. No reactions or emotional response whatsoever. You are basically becoming boring and uninteresting because you're not engaging. This method is typically used in relationships with narcissists because the narcissist feeds on the victim's response and uses it against them to make them question and doubt themselves, but it's an equally useful technique with addicts, too. Oftentimes, when a person is intoxicated or otherwise under the influence of a substance, they become more easily agitated and even aggressive because their filter is lowered. It's said that what a person really thinks comes out when they're drunk, and it isn't always such a pleasant picture. When he got drunk, he got emotional; sometimes that emotion came out in the form of crying (which really threw me off balance the first time it happened!), but more often, it came out as bitterness, anger, and frustration, which by themselves were fine, until they got aimed at me, which they did quite frequently. The first time he screamed at me, barely a month into our relationship, I was taken aback and dissolved into a sea of tears.

Yeah. That had stopped happening a long time ago. For a very long time after the tears stopped, the yelling back replaced it. I didn't want the fighting to escalate, but I also sure as *hell* wasn't going to sit there and let him scream, curse, and fling accusations at me. If he was going to hurt me, I was going to hurt him back. The truth is that I hated who I became from this point forward because I'm *not* a confrontational person. I don't yell and scream. I don't like fighting. It takes me back to places and times in my past that I don't want to revisit. However, the thing with an addict is that they *will* try to push buttons and elicit a response because that response makes them feel validated and in control in their inebriated state. It's a lot like dealing with a narcissist. The end-goal for the narcissist is always control, and they don't care who they stomp on to get it. While addicts are not generally overtly callous like that, they use the substance to escape their own demons to begin with, which paints a clearer picture of why control is so important to them. Addicts can be master manipulators, especially when it comes to ensuring that their chosen substance remains in constant supply. It also reaches into the relationships in their lives because any one of these relationships could potentially be the person who exposes the addict and lays down the boundaries that will ultimately make it more difficult, if not impossible, to continue using. Both the narcissist and the addict need control, just for different reasons. Regardless though, it can be extremely stressful dealing with an addict when they're actively using. They push, prod, and provoke until you reach your boiling point and then use your emotional reaction against you. I really had to learn this the hard way with him. For years I fought back. I "defended" myself, even though I had nothing to defend myself *for*. I *explained* myself even though I didn't owe him anything. I **engaged** him, which was exactly what he wanted. He was angry, so he wanted to make someone else angry. He was hurting, so he wanted to make someone else hurt. He was resentful, so he wanted to make someone else feel that way. I was always the one immediately closest to him, so I was the target most of the time. He also knew that I'm a naturally sensitive person. I'm deeply empathic. It's both a blessing and a curse, but he knew that in being so, I always consciously tried to understand how he was feeling and why. I tried to be supportive.

When I suddenly started fighting back, it caught him by surprise because it meant he suddenly didn't have the same level of control that he had become so used to having in our relationship, and his first reaction was to use it against me by accusing me of being "mean." I got that a lot. I was "mean" when I dared to react to something terrible he said to or about me. I was often met with "Sweetie, it was a joke. Relax" or "I didn't mean anything by it. You're so sensitive" (Gaslighting rears its ugly head!). I'm sitting there upset and hurt, but whatever he said was "a joke" that I was just overreacting to. He was the one who had been hurtful or malicious, but *I* was the one who was wrong for having the nerve to react with any kind of emotion to something that I "should have known" was a joke.

Let's just get something straight here — once the other person reacts with any emotion that isn't positive to something said to or about them, it's not a joke. There's nothing funny about someone who is supposed to love you causing you pain, and it's even more disgusting to be then manipulated because you're reacting as any normal person who was just hurt by someone would. It becomes easy to see the vicious cycle that this can become and how quickly and easily it can wear down the victim. I may have appeared to be full of sudden kinetic and emotional energy, but after months and years of it, inside, I was eviscerated. Interestingly though, it was at the point that I realized how depleted I was inside that I sort of sagged into what I thought at the time was defeat, but soon realized was actually a tool that would allow me to get through these constant verbal drain-circlers without collapsing. I didn't know what it was called at the time, nor had I ever even heard of it. It wasn't until I came into one of the social media support groups and started reading the posts from other members in similar situations that I came to learn what grey-rocking was, which in turn made me want to learn more. To say I was surprised when I realized that this was what I was already doing would be an understatement of massive proportions. "*How could this possibly work?"* I thought to myself because even lack of response seemed to further incite my ex's need to provoke from my experiences. That's the thing, though. Grey rocking isn't a lack of response. It's a *detached* response. No. Emotion. At all.

Now, before you protest, yes — it is much easier said than done at first. It takes practice. After all, if you've been going back and forth with someone for months or even years in high-voltage emotional firestorms, to suddenly be able to shut it off and basically go cold seems not just unlikely but impossible. It's really not, though. Keep in mind that the addict who is poking and prodding you is trying to provoke a response. What would make this effort utterly and in all ways unappealing enough to him or her to stop trying? Total lack of acknowledgment of anything they're saying, and worse (for them), keeping your responses mundane and without any kind of emotional foundation or fuel whatsoever. That's why I would respond to him by saying, "If you say so," or just breezing over his efforts to engage me by telling him goodnight and reminding him to take out the garbage. Boring. Every day. Completely flat. It's tough to instigate a fight that way. They can try -- and they will, but if you remain completely grey (like a rock, hence the term " grey rock"), they will eventually get tired of trying, and if you're lucky, they'll even get bored; so bored that they decide it's not worth the effort to keep trying to get a rise from you at all. This sounds idealistic, and it can also seem to be at first. Chances are, at least the first few times you attempt to go grey rock, you may very well slip and wind up reacting to them. That's okay. This is by no means an easy practice. You're trying to train yourself not to respond to what is often a direct personal emotional attack against you. Anyone would react. It can be challenging to remember that they are doing it *for* the reaction, but once you have that solidly in your mind, it becomes much easier because you're taking away their entire reason for coming at you. You're taking away the reaction. Most people wouldn't want to bother engaging with someone who they perceive as boring and unresponsive, and that's exactly the goal you're aiming for. *I don't want to be **boring***, you might argue, and under normal circumstances, no, of course you wouldn't want to be boring. I said it once before, though, and I'll repeat it — this situation is anything but normal. You're trying to manage with someone whose behavior is severely impacted by a toxic substance that alters the brain's chemical makeup. They aren't the person you thought you knew. In truth, they may never have been, but that's getting away from the point. Would you want to try and engage with someone who holds no interest for you at all? Of course not, and even intoxicated, neither does the addict. They want the blaze. They want the explosions. They want *control.*

For the longest time, I couldn't figure out why the people passing by on the sidewalk wouldn't yell and scream back when he would lean over my deck while drunk and start yelling and trying to instigate with them. Here's a perfect stranger yelling at them for no reason other than that they were doing something that bothered him (Like the woman he yelled at because she was walking down the sidewalk talking on her phone. He felt it was "disrespectful" to the neighborhood. Ooookay.). Why weren't they reacting? Then one day, before yanking him back inside trying to get him to stop, I decided instead to watch. It was quiet for a few minutes, and then suddenly off he went. I peeked at the sidewalk and saw a young guy with a phone in his hand, and there was music coming out of it. It wasn't so loud that it would've scared the birds away, but it was loud enough to be heard, which clearly ticked him off. So sure enough, he started yelling. I watched, waiting for the guy to yell back, but he didn't. Instead, he just waved at him. He yelled some more, raising his voice to the point where *he* was the one disturbing the neighborhood, and I worried that a few more minutes of it might find me with the police on my deck as well. Again, the guy just waved, and I even heard him say, "have a nice day, dude." I waited for the inevitable movement towards the stairs leading to me grabbing him by the shirt before he could fly down to the sidewalk and into the guy's face, but instead, he did something I had never seen him ever do before.

He stopped.

He grumbled, he shook his head, and he stopped, and I realized that he stopped because he wasn't getting a reaction from the guy. I continued to watch, sucking in a hard breath when the guy stopped at the opposite side of the building to lean down and tie his shoe. I expected that to be the moment he leaped back to it, but still, he didn't. He just put his cigarette out, flicked the butt over the railing, and turned and went back inside. I couldn't believe it.

This is perhaps an abridged example of how grey rock works. The basic premise is there, though. He yelled, he didn't get the reaction he wanted, and he stopped. Obviously, this will be considerably more difficult when you're dealing with someone with whom you have a close personal relationship. This was a stranger, so he had no problem ignoring the drunken rant being spewed at him. He couldn't have cared less, but obviously, you're likely and understandably going to. That's why going grey rock is hard, but it's also so worth it for the sudden realization that your addict isn't trying to instigate with you the way they used to, or attempts at engaging you in arguments are far briefer than they used to be. If you do engage, you're keeping the conversation so "every day" and mundane that they've lost interest in trying because it isn't getting them the explosion they're looking for. You're not feeding the beast, so it's going to find its source some other way. Unfortunately, with my ex, he was also feeding his need for confrontation by getting into fights with random people on the street and coming home all cut up and bloody. Obviously, that's not how most people are going to react. My ex had some pretty major anger issues that he hadn't dealt with, and that was his way of getting them out, I guess (In rather "Duh" like hindsight, this also should have been a HUGE red flag to me. People don't just get into brawls with strangers while out for a walk.) That didn't make it any less alarming and scary. Again, though, that's neither here nor there for this discussion. The point is that if you're not providing that source, they're going to give up trying with you.

This leads to the obvious question of *how?* How do you shut off when someone is coming at you? First of all, it's important to understand that this isn't necessarily appropriate in *every* situation and may not work in every situation. The first situation that comes immediately to mind is violence. If you're involved in a relationship with someone violent, grey rocking is not likely to help you; it may incite further violence. For example, even though this is a technique typically used to avoid engaging with narcissists, it is absolutely *not* recommended that you go about this approach with a malignant narcissist. These people are dangerous and have no regard for the well-being of anyone else. At the risk of being frighteningly blunt, they won't think twice about punching, throwing things at, and even stabbing someone when they're enraged, gender irrelevant. If you're involved with someone violent, you're in a situation in which you need to think about your safety first and foremost at all times. Grey rocking this person will anger them further, and that's the last thing you want to do. Please, use common sense with this technique and gauge your situation for the level of risk. The last thing you want or need to be doing is engaging behavior that will heighten that risk.

If you're not in a potentially dangerous situation, though, how can you utilize grey rock to be able to keep some degree of sanity amidst the chaos? It's easy to say "just don't engage," but it's much, much harder to actually do it -- or not do it, in this case.

We've already talked about the toxic person, in this case, the addict, looking for that conflict. Well, it's challenging to provoke an argument with someone who is giving one- or two-word answers. For example, in my case with my ex, "if you say so" was a simple, four-word statement that offered absolutely nothing... including an open door for his continued provocation. There's really not a lot you can say to such a flat statement because it's a pretty clear indication that you have no intention of engaging. That's not to say that they won't try at least a little bit more. God knows my ex did, but I also have to say that overall, the heated situations started lasting for far shorter periods of time than they had when I'd engage with him and get heated right back. Responses such as "uh-huh," "yes," and "no" also work because they don't invite return response. If anything, they almost shut down further conversation because of the sheer lack of active engagement, and that's the idea. Make your responses non-committal, and you're essentially yanking the match right out of their hand before they can even light it, let alone throw it at you.

Another natural tendency that you might not think of as encouraging continued provocation is eye contact. Eye contact strengthens that emotional connection because you're directly acknowledging them as part of your immediate space. Not looking at my ex was something I did with him constantly, though admittedly, most of the time, it was just because I really didn't want to look at him. Looking in another direction diffuses the tinder because you're not giving them that precious attention they're trying so hard for. If a person isn't even *looking* at you while you're trying to engage them, the disinterest is pretty clear. You're telling them without words that you're not going to engage in their attempts to instigate and inflame.

Fair warning: This could also bring reactions to the surface that you might not see coming. When I'd look away from my ex when he tried to start an argument, he immediately assumed and subsequently accused me of looking at a text message from some guy I was cheating with. My phone didn't even have to be anywhere near me. There were many times when he indignantly insisted that he *saw* my phone in my hand when it was actually sitting on the table next to me. If I wasn't holding it, I was at least looking at it, and it had to be because I was cheating and talking to whomever the latest guy was that he was certain I was cheating with. At first, this became enough to pull that reaction out of me simply because it hurt and infuriated me that he would think I even could cheat, let alone would. Again, though, I realized after a while what he was doing, and honestly, even if he was absolutely certain without a shred of doubt that I was unfaithful, *I* knew I wasn't, so I had nothing to defend. That made it easy to stop even acknowledging him when he tried to use it as a means of poking me into an argument. Look away. Focus your attention elsewhere. Pull that emotional connection away. It's a lot like a human being — if you don't feed it, it will die. If phone and email are options, use them. They make grey rocking a hell of a lot easier.

Don't "enlighten" them. You may feel tempted to hiss at them that you're blocking them out. Yeah, don't do that. I know it's tempting as hell to tell them you're deliberately ignoring them, but the whole idea of grey rock is to become completely uninteresting to them so that they stop trying to provoke. If you *tell* them that's what you're doing, you've shown them your hand before the game even starts, and they can and will try to then find ways to manipulate you using what you've just given them. You're handing them the weapon to stab you with. Instead, start telling yourself that you're dealing with a stranger because really you are. You don't know this person who's coming at you and trying to pull you into an argument by saying terrible, hurtful things. The person you knew and loved would never do that! This is a stranger. Start training your mind to look at them that way. It's easy not to engage or even care with a stranger, right? The caution here is that you want to be careful that this doesn't become a wall for you. While it can be very effective in shutting down the addict's attempts to engage you in confrontation, you want to be sure that it doesn't become an issue in those relationships you have with people you know you can trust. Talk to them. Be transparent with them. Tell them what you're trying to do. This way, you're not cutting off your nose to spite your face.

Mindfulness and self-awareness become critical when trying to grey rock with someone because you can become lost in the self-protective barrier. The whole point of grey rock is emotional disconnection, but if you're not careful with it, you can wind up separating from relationships you don't want to lose. Don't lose *yourself* trying to lose the addict's attention. If you feel like you've started pulling away from your feelings and feeling disconnected from loved ones, please seek guidance and help to get back into a healthy place. Protect yourself from complete detachment. A good therapist can be so invaluable in situations in which you're trying to detach from a toxic person. They can help you maintain a perspective of what (and who!) is truly important to you in the face of concerted efforts to pull away from the toxicity of the addict in your life. There is no way I would have had the strength to maintain grey rock with my ex after a while without Kathryn's support and encouragement. When I started feeling guilty, she reminded me of *why* this was necessary and how important it was for me to take care of myself in this abusive and destructive relationship I was caught up in. The less I gave him, the less he'd have to throw back at me. If I didn't grease the fire, it would eventually have no other option but to die out.

Codependency can make grey rock considerably more difficult. This shouldn't come as a surprise by this point. Guilt can be a brutal manipulator in its own right, and unfortunately for codependents, it's also a given. Again, I can't emphasize enough the importance of therapeutic support here. It's so important to remember that what you're doing is self-preservation. You *have* to protect yourself. I get that it's painful. I really do. It's so hard watching someone you care about change and become someone you not only don't recognize but don't even feel emotionally safe with anymore and be completely helpless to do anything about it. It's a terrible feeling, but this is the point at which you have to start taking care of yourself. Grey rocking with an addict can be a strong way to do this once you get the hang of it. Confide in *trusted* loved ones. Don't keep the frustration, desperation, and pain bottled. Just don't let your addict see or know about it because your emotions aren't safe and will very likely be used against you in the mental state that they are in. It's a punch in the gut, but once you've accepted it for what it is, it gives you the ability to begin releasing yourself of all of that responsibility for protecting and "rescuing" them that you've been unfairly carrying around on your own shoulders for so long.

I can tell you that while I initially kind of "fell into" the gray rock space with my ex, it wasn't always easy to maintain it. He knew how to hurt me and piss me off, and he went right for it when I didn't respond to him. There were times when I had to clench my jaw to keep from reacting to him. He knew what my buttons were. He knew what my triggers were, and he knew how to hit them just hard enough to hurt. In the beginning, that hurt was all I needed to fly off into a yelling fit right back at him even though logically I knew it wasn't going to get me anything but a headache (that much was a guarantee!), yet I still struggled with this. *I* felt guilty. In all honesty, I don't know if I was feeling that way because of my codependency, because I hated that I could become such a person since it wasn't who I was nor who I wanted to be, or a bit of both. I'm inclined to believe it was a little of both. It was difficult for me to be that angry. I don't like confrontation. I grew up with a lot of it, and I have a strong aversion to it now. I just don't like being an angry person, let alone an angry person who reacts out of vindictiveness. I freely admit that I said things to him in the heat of some of our fights that I regret and wish I hadn't. I took shots at him that I'm not proud of, but if you've had any kind of lengthy involvement with an active addict, you know that it can often get to the point where you'll say or do anything to get a little bit of peace and quiet. Everyone has their boiling point, and I knew where and how to hit back to make him reel just enough to shut him up, at least for a little while. What was interesting (though not surprising) to me was how he'd react when I did it – like *I* was this horrible, cruel, heartless person – and again, that's exactly the purpose of the addict trying to engage the other person to begin with.

Confrontation is excruciating for the codependent because it rips at that wound -- that wound of not being enough. Whether or not we've even done anything wrong -- and most of the time we haven't -- we still take this confrontation as further validation that *we* must be "bad." We want to fix it. We want to mend it. That's why grey rock can be so difficult. It flies in the face of any efforts to bandage the problem because it just doesn't acknowledge it in the first place. In a healthy relationship, this is typically unnecessary because people can work things out civilly and respectfully. Civility and respect in a relationship with an active addict are infrequent, to say the least, though, and their absence makes keeping the peace that much harder. We want to. God knows we want to. We want to find that one thing to say or do that will suddenly somehow "breakthrough" to them and make them calm down.

It's not going to happen. I know that seems like a definitive statement -- because it is. It's not going to happen. The active addict suddenly having this lightbulb moment in which they realize how they're treating you and become apologetic and loving again is wishful thinking at best. Please don't torture yourself, holding out hope for it. While engaging grey rock with an active addict is by no means easy, waiting for them to have some kind of sudden and behavior-changing realization is going to be a hundred times harder because it's never going to be the reality. Slips happen, and that's okay, but if you can get to a point and a place in which you're able to engage grey rock with the addict in your life consistently, you're going to find that peace becomes far more prevalent, as will your ability to see and recognize their ridiculous and manipulative behaviors for exactly what they are -- desperate attempts to maintain control so that their own need can continue to be fed without any kind of threat. Lean on the safe and trusted people in your life. Let them know what's going on and what you're doing and let them give you strength. Doing grey rock is really hard, especially at first. The last thing anyone wants to have to do is 'tune out' someone they care about, but the confrontational addict really gives you no other choice. Trust me when I tell you that you will find unexpected strength in recognizing the crap for its stink, so to speak, and shut the problem down before it has the chance to become one. I know it may feel like you're ignoring them, but please ask yourself — what are they giving you that's worth acknowledging? This is the consummate example of detaching with love. No one should have to be forced to detach from someone they love because that person is toxic and abusive, but if you're in such a relationship, grey rock is a strong way to do so – and remember; you're not "doing this" to them. You're having to do this because of what *they* do to *you.*

Please remember that and be kind to yourself.

You're getting enough crap already.

14

September 2020

Tears poured down my face. I was drowning in thoughts of him, and the pain was as sharp as it had been in the days and weeks following my cutting off all contact. There was a commercial playing for a home loan company on the television, which opened with talking about the importance of being home and having a home and being as sharply aware as I was that he was homeless, I was suddenly wracked with body-shaking sobs. It had been nearly a month since I cut him off, and yet there I was vehemently fighting to resist an urge to reach out to him that was a strong as it had been in the days following the cut-off.

"What's *wrong?!*"

My friend Paula's voice sounded alarmed. I had called her in tears, struggling to fight the consuming push to call him, and I was still in tears when she answered, so my attempt at saying "hello" came out as little more than a rapid-fire series of choked breaths. She and I had connected in one of the loved ones of addicts support groups I had joined on social media looking for support, and she had quickly become someone with whom I found strength, courage, and comfort. She was also in a relationship with an alcoholic — for far, far longer than I had been with my ex, so she knew what I had been dealing with and vice versa. She had become an invaluable friend and confidant. I was so immensely grateful for the kindness she had shown me the first night she reached out to me after I had written an incredibly raw post in the support group about something that had been going on with him.

"I miss him. It hurts so much knowing he's homeless. I just want him to be okay".

I thought I had finally been getting past this. I had started feeling better, stronger. I hadn't been crying as much when I thought of him. Then I saw this commercial — this commercial that I'd seen a hundred times before, and I was consumed by emotion all over again.

"What happened? Are you okay? Did you hear from him?"

"No. I just… it really hurts tonight. I don't know why".

Yes, I did.

I was triggered. The commercial *triggered* me.

I felt it was important to devote a chapter to triggers because they are such a huge part of both trauma and healing. It's easy to kick ourselves when we give in to a trigger, but it's critical that we understand both the source and nature of triggers so that we can accept that they are *normal*. Like the pain of going no contact with an addicted loved one, triggers are a part of the process that we have to go through to get through. We have to allow ourselves to sit with the pain they bring because it's through that pain that we can begin releasing all of the toxicity that has been poured into us through the experience of trying to love someone with an addiction, especially if we struggle with codependency ourselves. The more we understand triggers and their place in the healing process, the better able we'll be to recognize them when we experience them and respond to them in healthy ways.

A trigger is an excruciating part of healing from trauma. Emotional triggers are like internal minefields that erupt when something familiar touches them. They are hypersensitive and highly reactive sore spots within us that are activated by external experiences. Without triggers, healing would likely be a far easier and less excruciating process, but those sharp little pinpoint memories prod at our most sensitive places. The commercial for home loans is a trigger for me because I know that he is homeless, so hearing about people having and getting homes was painful because it made me think of him. That inner minefield was set off, and I fell apart. One of the worst parts of triggers — aside from the pain, of course, is that anything can be one. I certainly didn't expect that something as innocuous as a television commercial would send me into a tidal wave of tears, but it did. Even as I write this book three months later, I still have to mute it when it comes on because the intensity of the feelings of sadness, worry, guilt, and grief I feel when I hear it is just too much.

Despite anything else, I do still care about him, and even miss him or at least the man I thought he was. As I write this, I have no idea where he is or how he is, if he has found a place to stay, or even if he's still alive. The last thing I heard was two weeks ago when his mother told me he had been living on the street, and that in and of itself was probably the single biggest trigger I've experienced since I walked away. That same conversation was the one that led to her giving me the number of the hotel he had gotten himself into, which is why I shocked the hell out of myself when I deleted it without even having used it. I've been honest throughout this book, and I'm not going to stop now. I *do* still think about him. I *do* still miss him. I *do* want to hear his voice and know he's okay, and while the consensus of the people in my life is that I should be relieved that he's gone and not care about him one way or the other, that's just not the way I am. I spent four years with this man and was engaged to him for two of those years. I was intimate with this man. I lost a child with this man. Just suddenly not caring wasn't a possibility. The thought of him living on the street was emotionally overwhelming for my heart, and that commercial reminded me that that's where he was.

I noticed too that my reactions to the commercial were always different but also always consistent with the stages of grief. Sometimes I'd become upset. Sometimes I'd get angry and even flip it off or curse it out loud. Sometimes I'd just mute it and look away or quickly change the channel. The anger was shocking to me. I can't say that giving television commercials the middle finger was something that I made a practice of, but the commercial just seemed to set me off. It ran constantly, and every time it did, I became a little angrier. A little more bitter. I'd find myself telling it to shut the (expletive) up, but it wasn't the commercial I was saying it to, even though it sure felt like it was. I was cursing at that tender place inside me that still cared so much about him and his well-being. I didn't *want* to care. I didn't want to think about him and wonder and worry about whether or not he was okay. He wasn't making any effort to contact me, which honestly surprised me initially because normally when I went silent on him, he always kept trying to get me to talk to him again, so this was a 180° change from the norm. Then again, the man *was* homeless, so he had bigger concerns than trying to reach me.

Still, that codependent place inside me felt abandoned, even though I was the one who left. Go figure. I was frustrated with myself that I was being triggered. It was illogical thinking, but it was how I felt, and I had to work really hard to redirect my thinking to be a little kinder to myself. My emotions were still a lot rawer than I wanted them to be after three months, and the fact that I was still able to be triggered was evidence of that. This commercial was not the only trigger I discovered I had. There were (and still are) certain television shows that I couldn't (and still can't) watch anymore even though I still liked them because they were shows that he and I always watched together, and now they were too painful. They were triggers. A foot pressed down on one of those super-sensitive internal minefields then quickly pulled back. It was just enough to send me spiraling into tears, but not enough to break me down completely — at least not yet. I know the risk was still there because let's face it — three months is not a long time, especially not after four years.

At the point at which I'm writing this, it has been four months since I last spoke with him, and though I'm unquestionably feeling better and stronger than I was two months ago, I still find myself being triggered. This is the longest he and I have gone without talking in more than four years. I would be lying to both you and myself if I said that there isn't a lingering sense of emptiness inside me where he used to be. It's that emptiness that gives strength to triggers. I still feel those twinges when I think about him. I still feel that ache and the longing for everything I had seen with him in the beginning. I still catch myself circling through memories of happier times and even the intimate times.

Memories not only can be but are one of the most significant triggers in healing from emotional trauma because they scratch and rub at that raw wound perhaps more than any other trigger can. They're that representation of what could have been, and that's painful. While I'm aware of some of my triggers, others have caught me off-guard. I can't watch any commercials that have to do with babies because I become angry and resentful both that I lost my own child and that I spent four years waiting for him to get healthy so we could have a family together. I know that I can't blame him for my determination to wait and hope. That was my choice, and as such, the only one responsible for it was me. It still doesn't keep me from feeling anger and resentment that the vodka was always his priority. I also have a difficult time being happy for loved ones if they announce that they're pregnant. That's not something I'm proud of. I never want to feel jealousy for a friend who is experiencing joy, but that's, unfortunately, the place my heart is in right now because I didn't get that chance myself. Sometimes I just sit in my new place and look around, and the silence triggers me, and that's a very odd sensation because silence should be something that I welcome after four years of chaos. That's just it, though. I became so familiar with chaos and anxiety that it's like now my system doesn't know what to do with silence because it's waiting for and expecting that other shoe to drop as it always has before.

Triggers can present in different forms. Dreams, for example, though, if they're triggering, chances are they're more nightmares. I've had dreams about him here and there over the last few months, and I always wake up feeling grief-stricken and raw all over again. Conversations with others can be triggering. Music can be triggering. I don't listen to the radio, but even if I did I know I could probably breathe easily in the knowledge that the chances of hearing our song would be slim because it's an older song now -- an 80s song is "old." Geez, now I'm really dating myself, here! I also know, though, that if I did hear it, I'd likely dissolve into tears because hearing it would bring back memories of the beginning of our relationship before the rose-colored glasses finally fell off. Triggers are merciless because they provoke our most vulnerable places, and there's nothing we can really do except push through them and the pain they cause. Even though I absolutely adore her, talking to his mom is a trigger because I know she will tell me how he's doing, and the reports have yet to be positive. It hurts my heart that he's struggling, and I can't help him, thereby leaving me feeling anxious, emotional, and helpless. *Triggered.*

I'll share a particularly unexpected trigger with you.

When I left, I already had a new place waiting for me in New York. My mother had been kind and generous enough to view a place for me since I was still out of state, and I trusted her judgment when it came to these things, so whether or not the place would be mine would be made or broken by her opinion and feedback of it. After seeing it, she called me and told me that she thought it was a wonderful little place, and she helped me ensure that it was guaranteed so it would be one less worry for everyone since the relocation clear across the country was going to be stressful enough. She had met with the landlord and really got a good feeling from him. She asked him some questions, including what the neighbors were like, and he told her that except for the next-door neighbor, the neighborhood was quiet and that even the next-door neighbor really wasn't a problem --- that he just "had issues." Well, hell, don't we all?! Understandably, my mother thought nothing of that. Put that way, I wouldn't have either. As it turned out, however, saying that the neighbor had "issues" was an understatement of frighteningly massive proportions. Within minutes of moving in, it became immediately apparent that this man was mentally unstable, as he started hurling insults and threats at me and my father from almost the second we stepped foot inside the new place. Being someone who has studied mental illnesses for quite a while, I recognized Paranoid Schizophrenia in him pretty quickly, but the landlord insisted he was "harmless." What was harmless to him spiraled into a constant barrage of name-calling and death threats hurled at me from the voice inside the house next door. He would scream horrible names at me and threaten to kill me, and while he also threatened to kill pretty much everyone else and regularly ranted about the CIA and the FBI, for me, the trigger was the screaming and the name-calling. This was something that I had just escaped from after four years of it. My sensitivity to it was paper-thin. It got to the point where I stopped opening my living room window because I just wasn't strong enough to handle even the risk of hearing anything thrown at me from his direction. He became a severe trigger, to the point where I was afraid to leave even to go to my car because I feared being verbally attacked by this man. This was the point at which I started picking at my arm because I was just feeling so overwhelmed with everything I was trying to manage.

It's easy for people to say, "Well, just avoid things that trigger you." Come on, seriously. If it were that easy, trauma wouldn't be nearly as debilitating. Similarly, if it were that easy to avoid triggers, there would probably be far fewer addicts in the world. Why do addicts turn to their chosen substance? They're feeling triggered by something and want to make that pain go away. He was often triggered by something happening in his family, whether it was a fight with a relative or some situation occurring that he couldn't resolve. This would quickly spiral into that raw emotional place in him that he was too afraid to face, and that would be all it took for the vodka to reappear. I've said this before, and I'll say it again — I'm not by *ANY* means making excuses for him, but the bottom line is that triggers *are* a huge part of addiction. They're also a considerable part of codependency. For me, the most potent trigger is that feeling of helplessness — of not being able to rush in and "help" him the way I always did before and know that he was okay and safe. That is the ultimate codependent trigger. Being unable to take care of someone we care about who needs it is like sucking out what's left of how we measure our own value. That's what we're supposed to do. That's what we were put on this earth to do, and therefore not being able to do so is the most shattering trigger we can experience.

So, with all of this emotional provocation around us, how can we even begin to handle triggers when they happen? There's no one way to manage them. It really comes down to what works for you to help you feel stronger and steadier when a trigger happens.

The most important thing to remember when you find yourself triggered is to breathe. Take a few deep, slow breaths and remind yourself that *you're okay.* You're safe. What you're feeling is normal and okay, and it will pass. This can be hard to do when you're in the throes of what feels like a substantial emotional backslide, but it isn't. It's a natural part of healing from trauma. It's one of the ways the body and mind begin processing the events experienced so that they can heal from them. Triggers are extremely uncomfortable, but they're also temporary and typically fairly brief in duration. For codependents, triggers are often more challenging to maneuver through because they strike against that wound that has already been reopened. They can feel far rawer because of that wound. Clearly, they're also problematic for addicts to handle because typically, triggers are what drive the addict back to their substance — to make that discomfort go away.

While discussing triggers with my therapist during a recent session, she suggested moving to a different room in my home, and then looking around the room and acknowledging that everything in that room was mine. It may sound odd and even a bit awkward and silly, but there is tremendous comfort in acknowledging the here and now. It's called mindfulness, and it can carry healing a long way forward. Mindfulness is exactly what it sounds like — being in the moment and accepting what you're feeling as being both whatever that feeling is in that moment and being okay. 'This table is mine. This bag is mine. This is *my* dining room". Consciously acknowledging the present pulls us back into it. That's the point of practicing mindfulness. Mindfulness can be especially beneficial when feeling triggered for precisely that reason — it brings you back to the here and now, which in turn breaks the trigger's hold. An example of an excellent tool for mindfulness practice is meditation. The entire point of meditation is to bring you back to your center, and the only way you can be in your center is if you're in the present. We can't be in the future and being in the past throws us off balance. Meditation helps bring the racing heart and mind back to the middle ground in a calm and self-caring way.

Another critical element of mindfulness practice is that there is no self-judgment. Again, this can be difficult to do because our first instinct is to chastise ourselves for still having these strong emotions for, about, or over the other person. We tell ourselves we "shouldn't" still care about them. "What's wrong with me?!" we ask ourselves. We are our own hardest critics when the reality is that what we did was necessary to save ourselves from a toxic situation. Mindfulness is not just about being in the moment, but also being gentle to ourselves in that moment. We can't heal if we're busy beating ourselves up. Negativity takes up energy. Valuable energy. We've been through enough negativity already. The last thing we need or deserve is to be pelted by more negativity, especially from our own inner voice. It's important to be gentle and patient with ourselves, not just while practicing mindfulness but all the time.

Trauma is not a straight path to heal from, and we need our own strength and patience to wind around the twists and turns of that path to get to the end and finally feel healthier and more centered again. Practicing mindfulness is a healthy and positive way to begin that journey.

- **Rest.** Yes, rest makes another appearance. At this point, I don't think it needs much elaboration. I have discussed, and we all know the importance of rest for both the body and the mind and resting after experiencing a trigger can help them both to be replenished and essentially "reset." The sharp and intense emotions that come with being triggered will quickly exhaust and deplete the energy levels. Expelling that much high emotion at once, as happens with triggers, leaves us feeling like we were punched in the gut and across the face at the same time, reeling and unsteady. Let yourself rest. Your body. Your mind. Your thoughts. They all need rest after the emotional blizzard you just pushed through. Drink some water, maybe eat something to help those depleted energy levels, and then rest for as long as your body and mind need to. After I experience a trigger, the first thing I do is lay down, even if only for ten or fifteen minutes. I lay down, close my eyes, breathe, and if I fall asleep, great! It's essential to listen to yourself after you've come through a trigger. Your inner voice will tell you what you need, and quite often, it's rest.

- **Support**. As with going no contact, triggers are experiences from which you'll likely need emotional support afterward. I know I often did. Hell, at times, I reached out *during* the trigger, usually to my brother, who was quick to talk me through it and remind me that what I was experiencing was normal. Of course, I knew that, but logic becomes easy to lose sight of in such a heightened emotional state. Reach out to a friend. Reach out to a sibling. Reach out to your therapist if you have one. Reach out to someone you trust and feel emotionally safe with to help you process the trigger and the feelings and experiences tied to it. Talking about it will take more of the wind out of it.

- **Exercise**. We're hopping to the opposite end of the response spectrum here. While exercise may seem like the last thing you'd want to do after going through a trigger, it can actually be greatly beneficial in restoring both energy and mood. It's no secret that physical activity releases endorphins -- those "feel good" chemical messengers discussed earlier. Even a fifteen-minute walk can not only restore energy levels but also kick those endorphins into motion. It's like physio-emotional redirection, using physical activity to redirect emotional response. The body kicks it into high gear to help the emotions recenter by sending those wonderful little endorphins onto the field, and it's game on! Before you know it, the emotion is gone, and you're feeling grounded again.

- **Reframe**. Look at the experience objectively and reshape the negatives of it into something positive. Instead of getting frustrated and upset because you were triggered, remind yourself that this is part of healing and that that's what you're doing, so good for you! Much like boundary-setting, this too can take practice. The healing process is as exhausting as it is unpredictable, and it can be difficult for us to find ways to build ourselves up after we've been through so much. Reframing our negative repercussions such as triggers into positive responses can turn the entire picture of healing around and make it more about healthy personal growth than about the pain of what was.

- **Write it down**. Just as with journaling, writing down trigger experiences can help us both recognize potential patterns that can lead to them and develop healthy ways to approach and manage them. What was happening before the trigger? What were you feeling? Who were you with (if anyone)? *How* were you feeling (This is different than the question of "what" you were feeling. "What" refers to your emotional condition, whereas "how" relates to your body. Were you nauseous? Dizzy? Were you feeling really tired? What was happening *in* your body at the time that the trigger occurred?)? Write down as much as you can remember of the moments leading into the trigger. What you read back afterward can offer some real insights into things that you might not have ever expected to be triggers. Also, as with grief, writing it down gets the poison out. It releases the toxicity out of you and gives it a voice so it can be disempowered.

Triggers are a painful and unavoidable part of healing from trauma, and they can undoubtedly be destabilizing, leaving us spinning trying to get our balance back. The critical thing to understand about them is that they are both temporary and normal. Nevertheless, they are also very overwhelming, so once again, self-care becomes essential so that you don't wind up pulled under the emotional riptide. Everyone experiences triggers in different ways that are as personal for them as their traumatic event was, and therefore responses also need to depend on what is right for you. Reach out. Seek support. Acknowledge,

acknowledge, acknowledge. Say it out loud. Write it down. Rest. Practice mindfulness. Take care of and be gentle with yourself. You're healing. That takes time and, unfortunately, also sends you spiraling in and out of emotional currents. The more you understand about triggers, though, the better able you'll be to ride the tide and come out on the shore unscathed.

It's important to spend some time in this book talking about PTSD because it is a prevalently diagnosed disorder amongst those who have survived any kind of trauma. I didn't open the chapter in the way that I have the other chapters because there's really no way to caption PTSD. I also think that it's more important to get right into it so that you can get a thorough understanding of what it is, how it presents, and how you can heal from it.

PTSD stands for Post-Traumatic Stress Disorder. The title "stress disorder" may make it sound like some passing illness related to too much stress and the inability to handle it, but it's so much more than that. It's a mental disorder that develops in individuals who have experienced trauma, whether single-episode or long-term.

There are two types of trauma: acute and complex (also known as "chronic" PTSD),

Acute trauma is typically a single stressful/traumatic event or experience. Natural disasters, terrorist attacks, severe personal injury, miscarriages, car accidents, and even the death of a loved one are all examples of acutely traumatic events. They're not prolonged, but they are negative, involuntary, immediately intense, and intrusive. They cause emotional and sometimes physical injury, and while the experience is not repetitive, the after-effects often are. I can speak to this personally, as well. My best friend committed suicide nearly four years ago, but I still struggle with the emotional aftermath of both his loss and the fact that he took his own life.

Complex/Chronic trauma is the trauma caused by repeated and prolonged exposure to highly stressful and damaging events and/or exposure to multiple traumatic events. Child abuse, diagnosis of a serious illness, bullying, military combat, and domestic violence are examples of chronic trauma. The traumatic experiences continue to occur, keeping the adrenal and central nervous systems in a constant "fight, flight, or freeze" state and unable to find safety to begin healing. The trauma continues to pile on top of itself until the cycle of the experience is broken.

The definition of 'trauma' casts a fairly wide net. The DSM-5 indicates trauma to cover situations that include direct experience in/exposure to a traumatic event, witnessing a traumatic event, and even hearing about a traumatic event happening to a loved one. It goes without saying that people in roles such as first responders and firefighters are exposed to repeated and prolonged trauma just by the situations they work with daily, further compounded by the secondary trauma of working with the victims. The same applies to combat veterans – and sexual assault and domestic violence victims. By such a broad definition, it could almost be argued that everyone at one time or another has probably had PTSD, as you'd be hard-pressed to find a human being who hasn't experienced at least a single trauma over the course of their life. The kind of trauma that's indicative of a PTSD diagnosis is more pervasive for the individual experiencing it, though. While certainly, anyone would react with grief and pain over the death of a loved one, there's a difference in the intensity and depth of the grief from the loss of a loved one to suicide or murder than there is for someone who passes from old age or other natural cause.

Please do not consider this as my suggesting that grief and pain in any sense or presence are minimal. I am in no way suggesting a compare and contrast scenario. Grief is grief, and it's terrible. However, the kind of grief that typically leads to PTSD diagnosis is generally more prolonged, intense, and concentrated. Given this, it becomes easy to see how a diagnosis of PTSD could come from a relationship between a codependent and an addict, particularly if that relationship also involves abuse of any kind. Codependents tend to be more prone to emotional conditions such as PTSD just by their empathetic natures and trying to balance life with an active addict is no cakewalk, to say the least. As with so many other aspects of this kind of relationship and its impacts, PTSD can present in many ways; anxiety, depression, anger, self-isolation, and the most worrisome – suicidality. You might hear stories about a war veteran hitting the ground after hearing a car backfire because they are suddenly and immediately thrown back into their combat days, and it's not unlike that for anyone with PTSD. From personal experience, I can tell you that what might seem like the most meaningless and trivial thing can cause a PTSD flashback.

About a month ago, I was lying in bed watching television, and let's just say my mattress is not exactly a Sterns and Foster; more like a $100 job from Amazon. Needless to say, it pops more than a bowl of Rice Krispies, and I got used to it after a while. Imagine my surprise then when I rolled over, the mattress popped, and suddenly I found myself in a waterfall of tears without even having any idea why. I was shaking. I was riddled with anxiety and just utterly freaked out and couldn't get up and out of the room fast enough. It took me a good five minutes to get the tears under enough control to do anything, and I quickly called my twin brother, who is the more logical and level-headed of the two of us and really good at helping me come back to center when I'm emotional. I explained to him what happened and that I had no idea why and waited for him to tell me I was crazy --which I knew he wouldn't, and which I also knew I wasn't, but I sure as hell felt like I was getting there in that moment! Of course, he didn't, and instead was quick to gently remind me of what I had been through and just come out of and that given that, it made sense that I was now feeling hypervigilant. Logically, I know this. I know enough about PTSD to understand from a logical perspective what I was dealing with but remember — logic is easily silenced by emotion and trauma, and even more so for a Codependent. Had I been looking at this from a clinical or diagnostic perspective or hearing a loved one tell me about it, I would have said the same thing that my brother said to me, but it's easy to give advice and much harder to take your own. I was mere months out of a four-year long relationship in which verbal abuse, yelling and screaming, accusations, and chaos were regular features. As discussed in an earlier chapter, that keeps the central nervous system on constant high alert, and that alert is not going to instantly shut off once the situation has been resolved. I learned how to live on the defensive, and as such, I was always watching my emotional back, as it were, waiting for the next explosion to send my adrenalin levels hurdling back into overdrive. I'd had a flashback, one of the most common symptoms and experiences of PTSD. This is the brain trying to process the overwhelming amount, degree, and severity of the trauma that was experienced so that it can begin to heal from it.

Other symptoms of PTSD include:

- Memories of the event/events that are intrusive, intense, recurrent, and involuntary. In children, this can often present in dramatic play.

- Distressing dreams about the event(s) or aspects of it that leave the person feeling shaken and fearful upon waking up.

- Dissociative behaviors in which the person seems to be acting as though the event(s) is/are occurring in the present, and they are responding accordingly, as opposed to presenting with an awareness of being in the present and having the experience of a flashback.

- Marked psychological distress — depression, severe anxiety, fear/panic, self-isolation.

- Prolonged and persistent avoidance of people, places, and situations that could or do pose a reminder of the event(s). Isolation from loved ones in an effort to avoid coming into contact with the stimuli.

- Negative changes in self-opinion and cognition. Belief by the person that they are bad, or that no one can be trusted. New and obvious suspicion that the world and everything/everyone in it is unsafe.

- Distorted beliefs in the event's experience that lead the person to blame themselves for what happened.

- Dissociative amnesia. This is a mental disorder that causes a person to be unable to recall details of the experience or event accurately. Other potential contributing factors of memory loss/distortion, such as the use of alcohol or drugs, injury, and illness, must be ruled out for this condition to be determined.

- Significant and prolonged negative emotional states (anger, panic, shame, guilt, etc.). Inability to experience positive emotions/feelings.

- Marked loss of interest in previously regular activities.

- Detachment from loved ones.

- Sudden irritability and/or angry outbursts, often without provocation. This can lead to verbal and physical aggression against others.

- Reckless or self-destructive behaviors.

- Hypervigilance. Essentially, this means being on constant "high alert," with a significantly heightened awareness of surroundings.

- Exaggerated startle response ("jumping" at even the slightest stimulus, such as the way I did when my mattress popped).

- Difficulty with focus and concentration, which can often lead to negative repercussions in other aspects of daily life (such as work).

- Sleep disturbances, (I can attest to this one personally! Every night for the last four years, I've woken up at least once a night and am currently on a medication typically prescribed for people with sleep issues,)

- Loss of or marked change in appetite — eating more, eating less, or not eating at all. Difficulty with digestion. Nausea, and other gastrointestinal issues).

- Physical ailments — headaches, muscle aches, nausea.

According to the National Institute of Mental Health, for a diagnosis of PTSD to be made, the person must demonstrate at least one re-experiencing symptom, one avoidance symptom, and at least two arousal and reactivity symptoms for a duration of at least one month ("Post Traumatic Stress Disorder," n.d.).

These are some pretty heavy and life-altering symptoms to be experiencing day in and day out for weeks or months at a time! It can and will quickly wear on the person going through them. For the codependent who is already struggling with such an overriding feeling of not being enough, PTSD can be downright debilitating (though that's not to say that it can't be and isn't for people who don't struggle with Codependency. That's not the case at all!). I was diagnosed with PTSD two years ago and then again two months ago, and its symptoms are as mercilessly prolonged as they are overwhelming if not proactively faced and worked through with a trained professional. As with any mental illness, it's not something that you should try to "manage" alone. You're dealing with complex trauma. Your emotions are wounded and frayed, and your nervous system is exhausted and worn down from being in that constant state of heightened awareness. This is not like a cold or a cavity, where you shoot a quick fix at it, and it's all better. Trauma doesn't work like that. I saw a decided difference in myself between before I started working with a therapist and after. Even though I was still weak and hurting while working with my therapist, I had that safe emotional outlet in which I could get the toxicity out with someone who both understood trauma and its repercussions and knew how to help those struggling with it feel comfortable enough to be able to engage in treatment.

With the rather wide girth that the definition of trauma encompasses, it can leave questions about whether or not a situation would be considered traumatic. Let me answer this question so that there is no confusion —

If it's traumatic to/for YOU, it's a traumatic event.

Trauma is not the place for clinical quibbling. If *you* are severely and adversely impacted by the experience or witnessing of an event, it's traumatic. For example, while it may not have been to some, every time I witnessed him having a withdrawal seizure, it was traumatizing for me. Was it happening to me? No, but the effects of it on me were emotionally terrifying and devastating. I would have naturally assumed this to be considered secondary trauma because it wasn't happening to me directly. However, my therapist was quick to point out that although I wasn't the one having the seizure, I *had* to make decisions to help someone else experiencing a traumatic event. She said that the intense rush of adrenalin is exactly the same; therefore, I experienced first-hand trauma. She said this was why every time it happened, I'd just meltdown and cry before I did anything else once he was taken away by the ambulance. I couldn't react in the moment, but I had to get it out because the experience of seeing him on the ground convulsing, shaking, with his eyes rolled back was more than my system could handle, despite that it reached the point where I had already seen it more than once.

The secondary trauma for me was the stories he would tell me about his seizures and the subsequent injuries he'd sustain because of them, and the fights he would get into and whether or not he'd "won or lost." While I'm not seeing or experiencing them directly, hearing about these situations from someone I cared about sent my central nervous system into that same heightened state of anxiety and emotion. I'd get pictures in my head of him seizing and hitting his head when he fell, or punches being thrown back and forth between him and some guy he had encountered on the street whom he claimed tried to steal his cigarettes, and the twist of nausea in my gut from those images was emotionally surpassed only by the thought of him being hurt; cut, bruised, and bloody. Anyone would react the same way to such thoughts of someone they love in that position, or at least I assume they would. Just because that's what I think, though, doesn't mean that the same experience would automatically be traumatic for someone else. Trauma is a very personal experience, and as such, so are a person's interpretations of and reactions to it. In this crazy time when there's a pandemic so sharply impacting so many lives, many have been traumatized by it in one way or another. For me, however, being a natural introvert, I'm not affected by it the way others have been. For me, it has not been a traumatic experience. Conversely, having a mentally unstable next-door neighbor yelling, screaming, and throwing death threats around might not impact some people, but having just gotten out of the relationship with my ex, this is traumatic for me because it triggers memories of those experiences with him and the feelings associated with them. I can't speak to someone else's interpretation of trauma because it's *theirs.* God knows, having seizures the way he did would have been incredibly traumatizing for me, but they didn't seem to be for him. He brushed them off as no big deal.

Trauma is universal in that many people experience it, but that's where the similarity ends. Knowing what we know about codependency, it makes sense that the codependent individual is likely to experience PTSD following involvement in a relationship with an addict. Abuse would, of course, complicate this dynamic further, but either way, people struggling with codependency are very likely to wind up suffering from PTSD once their toxic relationship has ended.

While therapy is the ideal means of proactively managing PTSD, it may not always be possible. Certainly, with the current state of the world, the possibility of going in and sitting down with a therapist every week or other week is considerably lower than it would have been a year ago. Of course, there is always the financial piece. So, if you're not able to find and work with a therapist for whatever reason, you might be feeling like you're just indefinitely stuck with your symptoms -- but you're not. You can do things for yourself to work through what you're experiencing if you're unable to get into therapy right now.

- **Deep breathing/Meditation:** I know that repetition may seem like somewhat of a revolving door in this book at times, but it's because so much of what's being discussed in it cross-references. This is no exception. I spoke about deep breathing and meditation as a means of self-care, and it applies to working through PTSD symptoms, too. These grounding techniques have strong positive impacts on dopamine and endorphin levels in the brain, which in turn translate into and through the rest of the body. Bringing yourself back to center re-establishes the stability that becomes splintered when experiencing PTSD symptoms such as flashbacks and hypervigilance. It reengages healthy cognition and reminds the mind and body that they are out of harm's way and safe. Even five minutes of meditation can do wonders for the mood, and both deep breathing and meditation are intensely personal practices that are entirely self-care focused.

- **Self-awareness exercises:** Again, (I know, I know!) activities such as journaling can be immensely helpful in clarifying patterns and situations that can potentially lead us into being triggered. Are you triggered more when you haven't gotten enough sleep? Do triggers occur more frequently when things are stressful at work, or you've just experienced another life change? Monitoring your daily routines and moods can help you identify areas in which change might be beneficial to diminish the occurrence of triggers that lead to experiencing PTSD symptoms.

- **Self-soothing**: The term "self-soothing" usually conjures up images of infants sucking their thumbs to stop crying, but it can be effective for adults coping with PTSD as well. Now obviously, I'm not suggesting that you shove your thumb in your mouth (though hey, if that works for you, more power to you!), but what I am saying is that everyone has behaviors and methods for bringing themselves back to a calm place after something has upset (triggered) them, and this would be a situation in which to use them. Maybe taking a warm bath helps you feel better. Maybe going for a walk and getting some fresh air brings you back to center. Hell, maybe screaming into a pillow until you've forgotten what you're screaming about, and you notice the dog is looking at you funny helps you calm down. Whatever it is that brings you out of stress and anxiety and enables you to feel even-keeled again, as long as it's safe, do it! Human beings were given the ability to self-soothe for exactly that reason — so that we can help ourselves feel better when things are stressful or overwhelming.

- **Social/Emotional support**: This one should pretty much be a given by now. We all feel better when someone we love encourages and supports us through a difficult time. PTSD symptoms are brutal and working through them when triggered is draining and can feel very defeating. Let your loved ones help you stand when you're struggling with your PTSD. That's what they're there for. Reach out to them. Ask them for guidance and advice. Tell them what you're feeling and experiencing. One of the first things I always tend to do when I'm feeling emotionally overwhelmed is call my brother. Family. Friends. Coworkers. Even social media connections. They can all be hugely beneficial in helping you manage your feelings and symptoms, and chances are if you reach out to them, they'll be happy to do so.

- **Distraction:** This may seem simple, but that's what makes it effective. There are no complicated procedures, steps, guidelines, or directions. Just do something that will make you happy and pull your thoughts away from your current emotional state. What were the activities that brought you joy before the trauma occurred? What made you feel replenished and refreshed? Maybe now would be the right time to find a new hobby, something you try for the first time and discover you find tremendous pleasure in. For me, that thing was baking. I only just came into doing it about a year and a half ago, but it became an instant love for me. I love the processes, the distraction, and mostly the creative freedom and flexibility it gives me. It helps me forget the world for a little while, and I love that. You become entirely wrapped up in what you're doing, and before you realize it, the symptoms you were experiencing have subsided, and your mood is better. There are few things more satisfying than simple pleasures.

- **Physical activity**: Yup. Here it is yet again. Those endorphins play a mighty role in healing! Take the dog for a walk. Take a bike ride. Hell, dance around your living room to 80s music. (Personally, I find few things better for mood-lifting than 80s music). The more the endorphins move, the better you're going to feel. It really is that simple.

- **Cry:** *How is that positive?!* Well, I'll throw that question back at you. How is crying a positive response to stress and anxiety? What purpose does crying serve? It gets the emotion out, right? That's why we do it. So, it stands to reason that after a good cry, we tend to feel better, right? I know I do. Tired much of the time, which is also good because being tired promotes sleep, and we've already gone over the benefits of sleep for both physical and emotional state, but I digress. An emotion that is let out can't continue to affect us. If we release it, it can no longer hold us hostage. Let it out, let it out, let it out! If that's what your body and spirit are telling you they need, give it to them. It may suck during, but you'll feel that much better after.

- **Pet adoption**: Okay, let me just preface this by saying that while pets are *wonderful* sources of love and support; as anyone with a pet knows, I know my Lunabelle keeps me smiling on days when I want to crawl into a pint of ice cream and never come out, they are also living beings who need to be taken care of. *Emotional support animals* are vastly different from everyday pets and require quite a bit of documentation from their human counterparts and specialized training and certification to become legally acknowledged. Please keep this in mind before you go racing off to the shelter to adopt little Fuzzy Wuzzy with the plan of slapping a collar around his neck and telling the world he's your therapy dog. I don't mean that to sound judgmental, but far too often, we make demands and have expectations of our pets when it's we who need to be taking care of them. I don't care how depressed I am. My Luna always comes first (which is why I could be down to a box of baking soda and some butter in my fridge, but she'd still have 27 cans of cat food in the cabinet). With that being said, pets absolutely can and do make amazing emotional companions that we can rely on for unconditional love no matter what, and that's certainly a big deal when we're trying to heal from PTSD.

- **Remain mindful of your physical health**: It's easy to get caught up in the emotional tsunami of PTSD, but it's important to remember that such intense emotions can manifest repercussions in the body as well. People with PTSD are often more prone to illness because the constant emotional swings and intensity weaken their immune systems. Make sure you're eating well. Stay hydrated. Get up and move. Get as much rest (there's that word again!) as you can. If you have preexisting conditions, tend to and manage them. See your doctor and get a physical to ensure that everything is functioning the way it's supposed to. The stronger you feel physically, the better you'll feel emotionally. The two are inextricably tied.

As you can see, there are many ways to help yourself manage PTSD if you cannot reach out for professional help. It's not something that you should ignore or disregard because it won't go away. Trauma needs focused attention to heal. On that note, it's also okay to treat yourself every so often if you're having a down day. Have some ice cream. Allow yourself something from your Amazon wish list, Granted, I have to regularly stop myself from that "something small" turning into $300 worth of baking supplies, and I'm not suggesting that you spend $4,000 on a 90-inch flatscreen smart television, but something you really want, and that's expense won't cost you the equivalent of your next car insurance payment. Dye your hair. Watch a marathon of your favorite show. Pamper yourself a little bit. We all need that sometimes, and that becomes even more true when you're healing after being hurt. I used to struggle with this, feeling like I was being selfish. Then I realized that sometimes it's okay and even necessary to be selfish. It's that difference between selfishness and self-preservation that I discussed earlier. Self-care comes in different forms, and self-pampering every so often absolutely falls under that purview.

PTSD is pervasive and all-encompassing, a volatile emotional powder keg that's quickly ignited and extremely difficult to diffuse once lit. While not easy, it is possible to heal from it, but it takes a devoted and active effort. Therapy is the recommended means of managing it, but there are other ways to manage the symptoms when therapy isn't an option. Understanding the symptoms and engaging in regular self-care are critical practices for effectively maneuvering the jagged dirt roads of PTSD. As codependents, we are especially vulnerable to relationships that could leave us reeling in the clutches of this terrible and painful disorder and loving an addict will send us flying up that path, stumbling over our own feet to try and catch some semblance of balance even as we continue to trip. Please be gentle with yourself if you're struggling with PTSD. You're dealing with trauma, and that takes time, patience, and lots of self-care to overcome. Just as addicts are told in 12-step meetings, this too is one day at a time. It's not a race, and healing can't be rushed. You're in a position to change your entire life, but first, you must deal with the path in front of you. Coming through that pain will not only make you stronger, but it will also help to ensure that you're far more cognizant of red flags in the future and are confident enough to walk away from them to protect yourself.

I feel like I need to backtrack a bit, and for that, I apologize. I realized as I was finishing the last chapter that while I've talked at great length about codependency and addiction, one thing I haven't explored is how to recognize codependency in yourself or your relationship. I know I touched on a lot of what pulls the disorder together as a whole, but I think it's just as important to give you the actual lay of the land in terms of the signs of codependence and what relationships with codependents might look like to ensure that you're getting the fully informed picture.

I know I said much earlier in this book that codependency is characterized by one person being wholly devoted to a dysfunctional and one-sided relationship in which the object of their devotion is emotionally unavailable, making them and the relationship toxic. *"That sounds awful!"* You're probably thinking, *"Why would anyone want to be in such a relationship?!"*. That's a fair question and one that I've strived to answer as best I could throughout this book, but I'll do so again for the sake of consistency. The codependent is drawn to the "need" (i.e., the dysfunction) in the other person because it triggers an unhealed wound of need in them. The codependent has been given the message that they are not enough, and to be enough, they must take care of others in need. On its face caring for others is a good thing, but codependency takes that to the extreme.

So, what are the signs of a codependent relationship?

- Your entire sense of self-purpose is wrapped up in the care and well-being of the other person.

- You have a difficult time saying "no" to the other person (boundary setting). Even the thought of telling them no makes you feel guilty like you're doing something bad or wrong.

- You do things you don't want to do because you're afraid the person will leave you (abandon you) if you don't.

- You fear speaking up for yourself, so you stay quiet to "keep the peace" because you don't want to upset the other person.

- You feel compelled to take care of others, often at your own expense. You put the needs of others above your own, even if it means you wind up in a difficult or strained position because of it.

- You dismiss your own thoughts, feelings, and needs as "insignificant" or "unimportant" because that's ultimately how you view yourself.

  - You become panicked and fearful if the person doesn't respond to your attempts at contact immediately, automatically assuming you're being rejected/abandoned. I can speak to this personally. I did this with him in the early months of our relationship. I was so attached to the affection he showed me that if I texted him and he didn't answer me within 15 minutes, I flew into full-blown panic mode. I became convinced that he had lost interest and was ghosting me. (Paging unhealed abandonment issues!)

- You always give and make sacrifices but don't get a lot of affection or even reciprocity in general.

- You recognize unhealthy behaviors in the other person (drinking, substance use, etc.), but stay with them because you believe you can "love them better" and because you're afraid of losing them.

- You feel constantly anxious about the relationship and worry about whether you're taking care of the other person and keeping them happy.

- You have difficulty identifying and recognizing your feelings because you've become so enmeshed with the other person.

- You don't trust in yourself, and your value is wrapped up in what others think of you.

- You take "responsibility" or even blame for the behaviors of the other person.

It sounds like a painful and restrictive way to live, doesn't it? That's because it is. Codependency is a painful wound that's easily reopened and causes us to put ourselves last for the sake of the needs of others. We learn that this is what we "should" do because it's where our worth and "enoughness" come from, but that's not true.

Now, what about addiction? What does that look like? How can you tell if your loved one might be struggling with an addiction? Well, there are often red flags. The problem is that in our determination to "see the good" in them and love them so ferociously, we allow ourselves to overlook those red flags until we're already up to our necks. The first night I got together with him, he asked me to bring alcohol when I came to his place. Did I think anything of it? Of course not. Why would I? He just wanted to relax and have a good time. Okay. I don't drink, but whatever -- no big deal.

Riiiiight.

So, fine. That first night we had sex, and he drank. Then the second night, we had sex, and he drank. Then the third night, well, he just drank. The one consistency that always seemed present in the daily routine was that he was drinking/drunk. Still, it wasn't screaming at me. However, I was starting to feel a bit unsettled by his seemingly constant need to be in the bag. It wasn't until about a week into it, though, that his behavior changed in a way that was impossible to overlook. He had never screamed at me before, but he was sure screaming at me that night. I was hurt, freaked out, and just shocked. *This should have been the red flag I needed to run!* It wasn't, though. All I could see was him and how I felt about him.

Going back to the question of how to tell if your loved one might be dealing with an addiction we'll start with the obvious one – behavior changes. Does your loved one seem to "flip" like a switch? Fine one minute, raging the next? Or does he/she suddenly go from calm to a sobbing mess out of nowhere? Does he/she seem easily set off? Or maybe he/she seems distracted or preoccupied? Do they have unexpected and drastic mood swings? I've talked about how the toxins in the substances the addict uses alter the brain, and indeed, changes in behavior are crucial indicators.

Other signs to watch for include:

- Physical changes. Have your loved one's sleeping habits changed? Sleeping all the time or going days without sleep?

Having nightmares or experiencing night terrors; episodes of intense fear and screaming while still asleep? Have they stopped taking care of themselves and keeping up with their hygiene? Have they lost or gained noticeable weight over a short period of time? Do they appear haggard?

- Have they seemingly begun to neglect other obligations and responsibilities in their lives? Are they not reporting for work or frequently missing work? Have they begun to slack on paying their bills or even taking care of their children?

- Has your loved one started behaving recklessly or getting in trouble? Have they been arrested? Have they started having medical emergencies out of the blue?

- Are they using a prescription medication more than they were directed to, or hoarding medication? Have you started finding empty bottles or cans "hidden" around? (The hamper, under a piece of furniture, I even found a half-empty bottle of vodka buried under a towel that I laid down in the bathroom cabinet of my former residence for the cat, so she had somewhere soft, dark, and quiet to hide in). Do they seem to be being secretive? Have you caught them in lies that they then try to backpedal from and twist?

- Have they started asking for money a lot, or do they seem to be always out of it? Have you started seeing drastic changes in your bank accounts, with large sums withdrawn, possibly even regularly? Remember how I talked in an earlier chapter about my ex always asking me for "solids?" That was why. He was always out of money because whenever he got a little bit, it went right towards vodka, even if it meant he ran out of cigarettes.

Unfortunately, these signs can vary depending on the substance being used. Someone abusing alcohol might present with slurred speech, secretive behavior, loss of interest in what were once regular and enjoyable activities, heightened aggressive tendencies, and coordination issues. In contrast, someone using opioids (like heroin) is more likely to present as confused and drowsy, complain of nausea or be vomiting, have itchy skin, exhibit hostile behavior, avoid eye contact with others. They might wear long clothes to hide needle marks. You know your loved one, and you know what is normal for them and what isn't. Of course, noticeable and shocking physical changes are a clear indicator that something is wrong, but the signs can also be subtle, so you really need to watch closely and trust your instincts no matter how much they protest and refute (and they will!). The active addict's primary goal is to hide their addiction at all costs so that they always have easy access to it. They will go to any lengths to maintain their secret, and unfortunately, nothing is off-limits.

Natural progression would lead to the next question being, "How can I help my loved one? How can I approach them?"

That's a tough one. You have to be careful because once an active addict realizes that their secret has been discovered, they can become defensive, defiant, and even aggressive— anything to protect their ability to keep using. You have to gauge how receptive your loved one is to even discussing the subject before anything else can happen. Remember, they can't become sober unless *they* are ready and willing to do what they need to do to become so. We can push, nudge, yell, coax, bargain, beg, and yes, even manipulate all we want. It won't work. They will only become more defensive and probably accuse you of trying to control them. Remain aware of how they appear to be reacting if you decide to approach them with your concerns. They may or may not be willing to talk to you about it or even admit that they have a problem at all. Your options become far more limited at that point because you can't make them do something they don't want or are not ready to do.

Express your concerns *gently.* Don't come at them full force with accusations or trying to fling "proof" of what you know at them. No one responds well to that kind of approach. If your true end goal is to help them, that is not the way to do it. You want to encourage them to help themselves and show them support, not try to control their decisions and movements. Blame discourages open communication. Tell them you love them and are concerned for their health and well-being. They may not think or even realize they have a problem or may not be ready to admit it. If this is the case, there's nothing you can do. It's painful, worrisome, and frustrating, but you can't force sobriety. For reasons that only the addict knows, they feel that they need this crutch right now. We don't have to like it, and, naturally, we wouldn't, but we may have to accept it for what it is because we have no other choice. I spent years begging him to get help. He just wasn't ready, and at the point, I left he still wasn't. I had to accept it because there was really no other option.

If they *do* seem receptive, that's great, but don't be too quick to let your guard down. Encourage them. Applaud them. Offer to help them find appropriate treatment sources. This is often the first test of how willing and ready they really are. If you try to open a discussion about treatment options, and they shut you down or try to deflect, more than likely, they still aren't ready and probably just agreed to it in the hopes that it would get you to leave them alone. An ugly truth, but often a truth, nevertheless. I don't want to discourage anyone from helping a loved one in active addiction, but the picture must remain clear. If they feel they are being pressured or controlled, they are likely to say anything they think might get that pressure off. If that means telling you they'll go into treatment, if it means getting some peace from the matter, then they will. He made promise after promise about getting help. In four years of promises, he followed through once, and it lasted for about two weeks. He was doing really well on the medication that had been prescribed to him, he was working with a counselor, holding down a job, and I started seeing hints of the man I fell in love with for the first time in two years.

It didn't last. He said he didn't like the side effects he was experiencing, and within days of stopping the regimen, he was drinking again, and the cycle kicked right back up where it had left off. He just wasn't ready. Don't forget that at the core of this, addiction is the need to escape from whatever it is that they're unable to confront on their own. We all seek ways to make pain go away, some adaptive and some maladaptive. Addiction is a maladaptive coping mechanism.

You can also try having family and friends gather as an "intervention," but again, this could very well incite defensiveness in your loved one. I don't advocate this approach for that very reason. I get the thinking behind it. "Hey. We love you and want you to be healthy and well." but I can almost guarantee you that your loved one won't see it that way. They're more likely to feel attacked, ganged up on. What does someone who feels attacked usually do? They fight back. They resist. This situation is one in which the active addict *truly* has to be completely ready for change and sobriety; otherwise, the response will not be what was hoped for. Just don't set yourself up for disappointment by going into it with high expectations based on what you want to happen.

I'm not at all suggesting that active addicts are incapable of caring about the feelings and concerns of their loved ones. They absolutely are. I *AM* saying that unless they are ready to make that change and work towards getting and staying clean and sober, your concerns are ultimately going to go in one ear and out the other. What is intended to be love and support from you will be perceived as an attack by them, and that's the last thing you want.

Don't come down on them. Don't judge them. Don't try to bully them into quitting with threats and ultimatums. I went this route at one point. It backfired miserably and ultimately made both the situation and the relationship a lot worse. It can feel like a no-win situation because if you come down on them, they fight back and resist, but if you try to show them support and that you want to stand by them, they will use and manipulate it so that they can continue using without repercussions because it will feel to them like you're so concerned about standing by them that they can do or get away with anything. I do hate to paint it that way but hating it doesn't make it any less accurate. As codependents, we want to fix it; fix *them,* and they see, recognize, and latch on to that softness as the vulnerability that will allow (enable!) them to keep using without fallout. It's a difficult situation either way. This is where it becomes imperative to do two things: Don't enable, and don't try to protect them from the consequences of their choices and actions.

"Wait... what? How can you even say such a thing, knowing how codependency is?".

I don't say it without sadness; believe me. The hardest thing in the world for a codependent is not stepping in and trying to "help" and "rescue." God knows this is why I stayed with him for four years before finally breaking away. I wanted so much to be that one person who could help him, that one person who could finally make him want to get help and get sober (There is that codependent " stinkin' thinkin, again!'). I wanted to stand by him no matter what because I felt that if he just had that one person who would stand by him no matter what (uh... hello? His poor mother?!), it would be enough to make him want to get well. For him, this was easy street — at least at first. When I suddenly stopped trying to protect him from his own consequences, the picture changed quickly and drastically.

He constantly accused *me* of "changing" and said things like "It's the classes you're taking that are making you think this way" or "it's your therapist putting these thoughts in your head." That was one thing that always infuriated the hell out of me about him. I wasn't capable of having my own thoughts. They always had to have come from somewhere or someone else. I wasn't paving the path for him to keep using anymore, and he didn't like the discomfort of that. If he wanted to stay in a hotel, *he* was going to pay for it. If he needed cigarettes, *he* was going to pay for them. If he was still even a little bit intoxicated on a day when he was supposed to come to my place, he had to wait it out somewhere until he was completely sober. I ensured it by buying a small breathalyzer and making him test when he came in the door. He knew he had to pass if he would be allowed to stay. I stopped paying for Lyft rides for him. I wasn't trying to control him. I was trying to establish some boundaries for *myself* so that I could have some degree of peace and stability in my life again.

Emotionally, it was extremely difficult for me to do because I still loved and cared about him and wanted him to be well and safe. I couldn't let him see that, though, because I knew if he did, he'd know I still had that soft spot that he could poke at until he got what he needed. We can't protect them from the consequences of their actions. It doesn't help them, and it certainly doesn't do us any good. It's painfully difficult to watch them fall, but we have to let them. Be compassionate, but don't be naïve. Be supportive, but don't enable. Love them but stop trying to protect them from themselves. For me, the hardest thing in the world was to let him fall — and he did fall. Hard. I care deeply about this man. I saw and wanted a future with him at one time, so seeing him crumble was utterly heart-crushing. There was no resemblance to the man I fell so hard for five years ago in the man I saw in the months before I left. It felt like he fell after I stepped back and stopped rushing in to catch him, but the reality is that my shoving the pillow under him to keep him from hitting the bottom was just continuing to delay both the inevitable and the necessary. Of course, we don't want anything bad to happen to them, but they're adults. It's not like we're rushing in to catch a child who's about to fall off the monkey bars.

As adults, we're responsible for ourselves, including the choices we make and dealing with their consequences. We're not helping them by cushioning their fall. All that does is tell them that they can do whatever they want because there will always be someone there to clean up their mess. Again, not a child who's drawing on the wall with markers. Children get protected by adults. Adults don't need and shouldn't expect the same kind and level of protection from other adults. That's not healthy behavior on the part of the addict or the other person. As adults and codependents, we need to step back and separate as much as we can. We need to let them figure out their own lives and paths. I know how difficult that is. I really do, and the truth is that to this day, nearly three months after our last conversation, I have absolutely no idea how he is doing. That's the painful part of this whole thing — letting go, but we have to. To us, it feels like we're giving up on someone we care about, but that's not what it is. We aren't giving up on them. We're doing the only thing we really can do for them. We're stepping out of their way. They need to either sink if that's their choice or learn to swim for themselves. If they're already entrenched in the sinking, there's no reason we should or need to sink with them.

Please understand I am *NOT* suggesting that you just throw your hands up and give up on them. You love them and want to help them. Of course. What I'm saying is that if it's clear that your loved one does not want to get sober, and you've worn yourself down trying and waiting, it might be time to detach for the sake of your well-being. Weeks can quickly disappear into months and years when you're trying to stick it out with a loved one in active addiction, and it will take a lot out of you. I held on as long as I absolutely could with him and cutting off all contact was the last thing I wanted to do, but I was emotionally empty, physically, emotionally, and mentally exhausted, depressed, and struggling with what seemed like constant physical illness from anxiety and lack of sleep. I knew that if I didn't walk away completely, I'd never break out of my own codependent cycle of bounding in to try and save him when he was in a difficult place. I knew he had to do this himself, and *I* had to heal and work on myself. Those needs could not work in unison, no matter how much I wanted them to do so.

Codependent relationships are complicated as it is because we are functioning from that unhealed place inside us that's so desperate for affection and approval — to be 'enough' and we don't know how to feel that " enoughness" just being who we are. Unfortunately, a codependent involved with an alcoholic is a recipe for heartbreak because we are not loving from a healthy place. We're trying to love someone who is emotionally incapable of reciprocating because they are unhealthy as well. Their entire focus is on that substance, so they have nothing to give to anyone or anything else. If you identify with what has been described in this chapter, chances are you're struggling with codependency. That doesn't mean you're incapable of love. Not even a little bit. It *does* mean that whereas loving an active addict is never easy, trying to do so as an unhealed codependent is utterly and in all ways detrimental. I'm not saying you can't or even that you shouldn't, but I urge you to take care of yourself. You can't help them if they don't want it, but you can help yourself.

17

I don't think this will necessarily be one of the longer chapters in this book, but I feel I would be remiss in what I'm trying to do with this book if I didn't talk more about the grieving process a codependent will likely go through once they have separated and cut contact with an addicted loved one. Of course, I know that any relationship loss is going to come with grief. A loss is a loss, and they hurt. With codependents, though, it tends to be a far more intense experience. Whereas a healthy person leaving a relationship will feel sadness, disappointment, and other emotions associated with grief, for the codependent, it feels as though their entire world has come crashing down, and they're dying under the rubble. I can speak to this personally. I spoke in an earlier chapter about my friend Justin and how I reacted when he became involved in a relationship. Let me elaborate on that to paint a clearer picture of what I went through emotionally afterward.

Even though I hadn't been given any reason to think or believe that he and I were any more than friends, that's not how I interpreted his affection. Having come from a history of abuse and disapproval, here was this wonderful guy telling me he loved me and being affectionate and open with me, which told that wounded place inside me that I was *finally* enough. It was the equivalent of winning the emotional lottery. I clutched onto him and clutched hard. I became profoundly and intensely attached to this poor guy without him even realizing the can of worms he had just opened and dumped all over himself. With every bit of affection, every "I love you," every intimate moment he filled that wound a little more. I was finally complete, not because I had found that within myself but because his affection and approval were telling me so. With this being the case, when I couldn't reach him or when he didn't reply to me right away, I went into panic mode and obsessively tried to get some kind of response from him, fearing abandonment. I was utterly panic-stricken that that affection and approval were going to go away, and I'd be left by myself and back to being not enough. If this was how I reacted just by not hearing from him within 20 minutes of a call or an email, imagine how overboard I went when suddenly there was this new relationship in his life. How could he DO this to me?!

I don't think I'll ever forget the day I found out about her. It was nearly 20 years ago now, but I still remember it so clearly.

The reason I remember it so clearly is because of the severity of my emotional collapse. I *fell apart.* I remember sitting in my car sobbing uncontrollably like I had just lost someone I loved — and to my heart, I had, but it was more than that. He had *abandoned* me. I had been *abandoned* yet again -- *rejected* yet again. I was back to being not enough. I was so devastated by this perceived rejection and abandonment that I actually considered killing myself because the pain was so consuming and overwhelming that I didn't think I could take it, and I didn't want to. I was reacting to him like a girlfriend — you know that girlfriend from "Fatal Attraction?" I *hated* this girl. She hadn't done anything wrong, and I didn't even know her. All I "knew" (in all of my codependent stinkin' thinkin') was that she had taken him away from me. I was seething with animosity for this girl, born of jealousy and that terrible and overwhelming feeling of rejection that *she* caused. After all, had she not come into his life, he wouldn't have abandoned me.

This might have been a more understandable feeling had he and I been in an intimate relationship to begin with, but as far as I allowed myself to believe we had been. He wouldn't tell me he loved me if he didn't want to be with me, right? Meanwhile, I told the people in my life I loved them all the time without it ever meaning that I wanted a committed relationship with them. Never put that together, though. I couldn't. In my mind, this was completely different. He was *supposed* to be in love with **me**). It took me weeks to stop crying. I spent days in bed overcome with this relentless consuming agony. I tortured myself with thoughts of them together and happy. I cried quite a few times to a mutual friend of ours and was more than content to let her be mad at *him* even though he hadn't done anything wrong.

When a codependent loses the relationship on which they've become dependent, it's as if their world has come to a wrenching and grinding halt. Feelings of profound devastation overcome them, and that hole inside them has ripped wide open all over again and is relentlessly gushing emotional blood. Depression, isolation, and even suicidality are not uncommon, and that's why I felt it necessary to talk about it further. Obviously, this is not a normal or healthy way to react to loss, and that's because it's not coming from the same place normal grief after the loss of a relationship comes from. codependents grieve hard not from the loss itself but from that deeply wounded place that had been being fed by the relationship, no matter how dysfunctional it was. All it takes is those first few bits of affection to flip that codependent switch into high gear. They're all it takes to send us soaring into the elation of believing that we've finally found love and acceptance. We become willingly vulnerable because we believe it's safe to do so in this beautiful new relationship we've found with this wonderful person who accepts us for us.

All relationships change over time, though, including changes in the affection and how it's shown. Normal, healthy relationships tend to settle into that calm, consistent place after the initial fire has ebbed out, and with that change, the level of initial passion often cools down a bit as well. For a codependent, this signals the beginning of the end. Even the slightest change in that high-octane blazing fire the relationship started in means that the other person is starting to lose interest, and we have to try that much harder to keep them engaged. We can and often do become obsessive, driven by that need that had just begun being filled. Honestly, Justin would have had the absolute right to tell me where to go and how to get there. He knew a lot about my past, though, and he was just too decent and genuine to do something that. I'll always be grateful to him for being so understanding and caring about me as much as he did, even when I went overboard.

Codependency is as demanding on the loved ones of the codependent as it is on the codependent. They don't understand the emotional intensity, and though they want to help, they don't know how or what to do. It's much the same as comes with loving an addict. We want so much to help them get better, but we don't know how to. Much like with active addicts, codependents also can't be forced or pushed into getting help. First, they have to recognize their codependency; then, they have to want to heal it. Regardless of the condition, it's hard to admit having a problem. We feel broken and weak. We often become our own worst enemies. I know that that's why he always said he had his drinking "under control." The constant repeating record of "Sweetie, I'm fine" was as much if not more to keep himself convinced and in denial about how bad it had really become as it was to convince me. I'm not sure if there was much intention to comfort or reassure me behind those words. It became hard to tell after a while because it happened so often. For years I was in that same denial about my codependency. At first, I could use the reasoning that I didn't know I was codependent because I had never heard of codependency at the time of the self-created situation with Justin. Even after learning about it, however, I didn't confront it, and because of that, I continued finding myself in toxic relationships (Justin commented to me recently that at one time he would have poked at me about how I manage to attract toxic men, and while he said it half-jokingly, sadly he wasn't wrong). Even though I knew that working on this and getting to its root would help me recognize healthy relationships from unhealthy (toxic) ones, I was still too afraid to face that root because of the pain I knew would come with it. I allowed myself to be "content" (if you could call it that. Looking back now, I'd call it denial) with getting involved with these toxic men because I knew that if I just loved them enough, I could heal them – even though I needed some serious healing myself. How can the sick heal the sick?! How can the still bleeding help the wounded? That's what codependence is, though. We convince ourselves that we can give the kind of unconditional love that we were denied and in and by doing so, we can heal the other person and receive that same love in return, therefore fulfilling that emptiness in us as well. Hell, it's a win-win - except that it isn't - for them or us.

Realizing that you're codependent can be understandably jarring, as it reopens flood gates we may not have even been aware were built, let alone at risk of being broken. Remember, this is likely an old wound that has been worn at over and over, and if it was there before we even realized it, imagine how sore it's going to be when it finally tears open. It's like that final scratch – that hare trigger that finally exposes the skin that has been kept so viciously protected by the overlying wound all this time. There's no getting around pain that raw. That's why as unbearable as it will be, the best thing we can do is face that wound head-on and work to proactively heal it so that it can't bleed and continue to cause us harm anymore. Just as the addict is dependent on their substance, the codependent is dependent on the need to be needed. It's medicating the same problem with a different medication. Whatever else it is, it is intensely painful, and we have to face that pain to get through it. One thing I've started saying in my own healing journey is, "To get through it, you have to go through it," and as much as I wish it weren't true, it very much is.

There are therapists who are specially trained to work with people who struggle with codependency. They understand the wound(s) associated with it and that those wounds need to be safely and gently but thoroughly addressed if the person is going to heal from codependency. I urge you to seek them out in your area. I work with one, and she has been great. My former therapist, Kathryn also works with clients who struggle with codependency, and she was my lifesaver. Finding the right therapist is a game-changer. Truly. Therapy is critical if you want to heal codependency and be able to recognize potentially toxic people in your life (or who are trying to come into your life!) and set firm boundaries with them to keep yourself protected. There are also a lot of fantastic books on codependency. The most recommended one (and I also recommend it!) is "Codependent No More" by Melody Beattie. It was the first book to explore codependency and offer guidance on how to heal from it. Having read it, I can tell you that it offers helpful insight into this life-controlling condition as well as tremendous support and comfort through the personal stories that Ms. Beattie shares and the advice she offers based on her first-hand understanding of how crippling it can be.

So, what are some signs that you could be suffering from codependency?

- Needing others' approval for any decisions you make because you don't trust yourself and your instincts.

- Poor self-esteem/self-worth.

- Difficulty setting boundaries in relationships, romantic or otherwise.

- You're a people-pleaser, often willing to do things that make you feel uncomfortable because you fear anger, rejection, or abandonment from the other person if you say no.

- You're a caretaker, putting the needs of others before your own.

- You don't recognize or can't identify your feelings.

- Taking responsibility for others' actions and choices and making excuses for them when they behave poorly.

- Difficulty communicating in relationships.

- You take the opinions of others as a reflection on you.

- You need to have control because it makes you feel more secure and safe.

- Intimacy issues. This could be a fear of intimacy or, conversely, the constant need for it because it's how you're able to feel secure in the relationship.

- You bite your tongue to avoid the risk of confrontation.

- You're a "fixer," meaning that you always feel the need to step in and "fix" or "save" people you perceive to be in need, assuming that they can't do what they need to do for themselves without your help.

- You feel depressed or even hopeless, trapped in the relationship, but you're not sure why.

You can see how this would be a painful way to live, always feeling like you're at the mercy of others' needs and wants, to the dismissal and (self) discrediting of your own. There's absolutely nothing wrong with caring about others' needs; (compassion is an admirable quality!). It becomes a problem, though, when you're putting your own needs aside to tend to others, or worse, you've become so enmeshed in the needs of someone else that you don't even recognize your own anymore.

Think about your closest relationships, the ones in which you feel the most loved, accepted, and emotionally safe. What do they have in common? Trust. Open communication. *Mutuality.* Security. If you have this kind of relationship in your life, chances are you feel safe *being yourself.* You know that the other person loves and cares about you and accepts you for who you are without conditions or expectations. That's how healthy relationships should be. It's exceedingly difficult for someone suffering from codependency to have this kind of relationship because they always wonder why the other person likes them. They're so riddled with self-doubt and insecurity that they find it impossible to believe that anyone *could* love them for them.

I struggled with this 20 years ago in the early stages of my codependency. My poor friends constantly needed to reassure and validate me. I'd say it's a wonder that I didn't lose any of them but knowing what wonderful people they are, it's not surprising at all. They never seemed to mind or have a problem with reminding me that they loved me because of who I was. Over 20 years later, those same people are still in my life; only now I don't need that constant validation anymore, which makes those relationships a lot more comfortable for all involved.

What do healthy relationships look like?

- There is mutual trust between both people involved.

- Both people feel that they can communicate needs, feelings, concerns, and boundaries openly and safely, knowing that the other will accept and respect them.

- There is patience between both people and an understanding that everyone is different and will interpret and respond to situations differently.

- There is shared empathy. Both in the relationship can recognize and respond appropriately to the feelings and needs of the other. They can put themselves "in each other's shoes," as the adage goes.

- There is mutual affection and shared interest in one another and what's happening in the other's life.

- There is a mutual appreciation for one another. Each one appreciates what makes the other who they are, differences and all, and recognizes that those differences are part of what makes the other person unique and lovable.

- Each in the relationship is encouraged and allowed to grow in who they are. People change. In healthy relationships, this is both understood and appreciated.

- Ability to resolve issues in healthy and respectful ways.

- Openness, honesty, and respect. These don't really need explanation.

The differences between the two kinds of relationships are pretty obvious. Everyone deserves happy, healthy, and mutually respectful and accepting relationships. Codependents don't believe they deserve such relationships, and that's the ultimate wound that needs to be addressed and healed so that they can find these full and rich mutual connections and feel secure in their worthiness to have them. Codependency is consuming and painful, but it doesn't have to destroy you. Don't be afraid of the pain of healing. What's on the other side is well worth the work it takes to get there.

Part 3: Final thoughts

I'll admit, I'm finding it hard to bring this book to an end because it has really become my baby. But since the goal was to provide support and encouragement to those caught in the snares of codependency and addiction rather than to be the second coming of "War and Peace" it has to end somewhere. I've covered a lot throughout these pages, and I do not doubt that it all probably feels pretty overwhelming right now. Whether you were already aware of your codependency, or you've discovered yourself in it through this book, chances are you're already in a relationship with a loved one who is an addict, and that's probably what drew you here, to begin with. It really is a lot to handle trying to remain beside someone in active addiction because we love them, but we're forcefully faced with the reality that they have a demon that we can't do anything to help them vanquish. Throw codependency into the mix, and that reality becomes less truth and more challenge — a challenge that we are primed and ready to tackle at any cost, even if that cost is ourselves. Codependency is born of a place of deep and unhealed hurt. So is addiction. Codependency is the way that we try to exert control over emotional wounds that consume us. The same holds true for the addict. There are so many similarities between the two, but in this case, it's those similarities that make this a wildly toxic and unhealthy relationship regardless of the parameters (family, romantic, friend, coworker, etc.). Both have their reasons for being and staying in the relationship, but none of those reasons are healthy.

Relationships born of need are dangerous from the beginning, and I mean emotionally dangerous. Both codependents and addicts have needs and are driven from their cores by these needs. He was at his core a good person, but he had some deep and unhealed wounds, and he was driven to bury those wounds with alcohol. I also had some deep and unhealed wounds, and I was driven to fill those wounds by taking care of others I saw as being in need because that was how I found my own worth. This is all too typically how this kind of highly dysfunctional relationship dynamic begins. Neither sets out to be manipulative and destructive, but because both are emoting from this place of unresolved need, any relationship they get into is essentially going to be dominated by that need. It's a painful way to live on both sides. I've never struggled with addiction, so I would never presume to know what it's like. I saw what it did to him, and it didn't look pleasant, but it seemed like his wounds were far more painful for him to the point where he would do anything to make them stop bleeding. That "anything" was vodka, and he would go to any length to ensure he wouldn't have to give it up. It destroyed us. It destroyed him.

My codependency added to that destruction. I loved him, but it was from a place of need. I needed to be needed. When we came together, we exploded, and I was left with no choice but to walk away completely, even as excruciating as doing so was. That's what happens with codependency and addiction. We come together, we spark, we ignite, we explode, we fall to ash. If you're in this kind of relationship or are trying to get out of or heal from one, please know that what you're feeling is normal. It's okay that you love someone with an addiction. It's okay that you're struggling with codependent. *It's okay.* YOU are okay, and you will be. There are ways to heal and invite healthy and positive relationships into your life, but you have to have that kind of relationship with yourself first. That's going to take time and hard work, but I promise you it can be done. It's okay to ask for help. It shows your strength and determination to get better and healthy for yourself. It's okay to love an addict. It's okay to want to love them and keep loving them in the hope that we can help them. What's not okay is surrendering your health and well-being for the sake of caring for someone who not only isn't caring for themselves but isn't reciprocating back to you either.

Addicts are not bad people, but they are people who, while in active addiction, are unable to give the kind of mutual love required for a healthy relationship. It's okay to love them from a distance. Sometimes that's the only choice we're left with. Boundaries and self-preservation are hard practices to learn for us as codependents, but I promise you they can be learned and even mastered, and you're worth that effort. You deserve to live a happy, healthy, and fulfilling life. Active addicts must find their own way to happiness and health, and so must we as codependents.

I hope that this book has given you some reassurance and comfort, and even some information and resources that you can use to determine what your situation is and how best to help yourself. You've taken a huge first step already. Now, all you need to do is keep walking forward. "Easier said than done," you're probably saying, and you're right. It's not going to be an easy path, but there's an old saying — anything worth having is worth fighting for.

There's no single fight in this world greater or more worthy than yourself.

May you find peace on your journey, wherever it leads.

May you find your worth, and never forget how special and enough you truly are.

May you find yourself and love the person you find because no one deserves your love more than you do.

Resources

I wanted to provide a list of resources that readers can use to get further help. I hope that these can be of help to anyone who may need it.

The National Domestic Violence Hotline: 1-800-799-SAFE (7233).

- 24/7 hotline with trained professionals who provide support and resources to victims of domestic violence.

SAMHSA (Substance Abuse and Mental Health Services Administration) National help hotline: 1-800-662-HELP (4357).

- 24/7, 365-day-a-year treatment referral and information service (in English and Spanish) for individuals and families facing mental and/or substance use disorders.

National Suicide Prevention Hotline: (800) 273-8255. 24/7

- Hotline on which trained professionals provide support, resources, and crisis management to those in distress or who are experiencing suicidal ideations.

RAINN Sexual assault Hotline: (800) 656-4673

- Provides options and support to victims of sexual assault.

Crisis text line: Text "Support" to 741-741.

- Text based support for people struggling with crisis.

Al-Anon for Families and loved ones of Alcoholics - Automated meeting information: (800) 344-2666

The Trevor Project: (866) 488-7386

- The Trevor Project is the leading national organization providing crisis intervention and suicide prevention services to lesbian, gay, bisexual, transgender, queer, and questioning (LGBTQ) young people ages 13-24.

https://ovc.ojp.gov/help-for-victims/toll-free-and-online-hotlines

- Provides a list of resources for crime victims.

https://www.codependencynomore.com/resources/

- A list of books and other resources for help with codependency.

https://cptsdfoundation.org/2019/11/22/recognizing-and-breaking-a-trauma-bond/

- Information on PTSD/C-PTSD and trauma bonding

https://www.addictionsandrecovery.org/addiction-recovery-links.htm

- Lists of support groups, both in-person and online for various kinds of addictions.

There are also some great resources on YouTube that provide information and support for codependency, addiction, trauma bonding, and even how to successfully go and maintain no-contact. If you're serious about using no-contact for its true intended purpose to help you heal, please be mindful of videos that focus on how to use it to get someone back. They are giving extremely poor advice, won't do anything to help you, and actually are more likely to make both your situation and your pain worse. They may serve a purpose, but it's absolutely not the purpose of healing. Please protect yourself!

Citation

Brecht, M., & Herbeck, D. M. (2013). Methamphetamine use and violent behavior. *Journal of Drug Issues, 43*(4), 468-482. doi:10.1177/0022042613491098

Brush, C. J., Foti, D., Bocchine, A. J., Muniz, K. M., Gooden, M. J., Spaeth, A. M., . . . Alderman, B. (2020). Aerobic exercise enhances positive emotional reactivity in individuals with depressive symptoms: Evidence from neural responses to reward and emotional content. doi:10.31234/osf.io/8k5zq

Colon-Rivera, H. (Ed.). (2020). What is a substance use disorder? Retrieved February 13, 2021, from https://www.psychiatry.org/patients-families/addiction/what-is-addiction

Compulsion. (n.d.). Retrieved February 13, 2021, from https://www.dictionary.com/browse/compulsion

Demers, C. H., Bogdan, R., & Agrawal, A. (2014). The genetics, neurogenetics And PHARMACOGENETICS of addiction. *Current Behavioral Neuroscience Reports, 1*(1), 33-44. doi:10.1007/s40473-013-0004-8

Edenberg, H. J., & Foroud, T. (2013). Genetics and alcoholism. *Nature Reviews Gastroenterology & Hepatology, 10*(8), 487-494. doi:10.1038/nrgastro.2013.86

Leigh, H. (2019). Recognizing and Breaking a Trauma Bond. Retrieved February 13, 2021, from https://cptsdfoundation.org/2019/11/22/recognizing-and-breaking-a-trauma-bond/

McFarlane, J., Nava, A., Gilroy, H., & Maddoux, J. (2015). Risk of behaviors associated with lethal violence and functional outcomes for abused women who do and do not return to the abuser following a community-based intervention. *Journal of Women's Health, 24*(4), 272-280. doi:10.1089/jwh.2014.5064

NIDA. (2020, July 10). Drugs and the brain. Retrieved February 13, 2021, from https://www.drugabuse.gov/publications/drugs-brains-behavior-science-addiction/drugs-brain

Post-traumatic stress disorder. (n.d.). Retrieved February 13, 2021, from https://www.nimh.nih.gov/health/topics/post-traumatic-stress-disorder-ptsd/index.shtml

Price, M. (2008). Genes matter in addiction. *American Psychological Association, 39*(6). doi:10.1037/e517672009-012

Ramani, D. (Director). (2020). *What is "trauma bonding"? (Glossary of Narcissistic Relationships)* [Video file]. Retrieved February 13, 2021, from https://www.youtube.com/watch?v=kmB9fpHVd2o

Seltzer, L. (2015, July 08). Trauma and the freeze response: Good, bad, or both? Retrieved February 13, 2021, from https://www.psychologytoday.com/us/blog/evolution-the-self/201507/trauma-and-the-freeze-response-good-bad-or-both

Sherman, C. (2017, March 09). Impacts of drugs on neurotransmission. Retrieved February 13, 2021, from https://www.drugabuse.gov/news-events/nida-notes/2017/03/impacts-drugs-neurotransmission

Vitelli, R. (2018, March 08). How are substance abuse and violence related? Retrieved February 13, 2021, from https://www.psychologytoday.com/us/blog/media-spotlight/201803/how-are-substance-abuse-and-violence-related

Made in the USA
Coppell, TX
19 January 2022

71879743R00103